Memoirs of a Biker

Traveling the Long Road

by
Joseph McCloskey

Order this book online at www.trafford.com
or email orders@trafford.com

Most Trafford titles are also available at major online book retailers.

Printed in Victoria, BC, Canada.

ISBN: 978-1-4251-1021-5

*Our mission is to efficiently provide the world's finest, most comprehensive book publishing
service, enabling every author to experience success. To find out how to publish your
book, your way, and have it available worldwide, visit us online at www.trafford.com*

Trafford rev. 12/11/2009

 www.trafford.com

North America & international
toll-free: 1 888 232 4444 (USA & Canada)
phone: 250 383 6864 ♦ fax: 812 355 4082

Contents

Prologue. v
I. Maritime Provinces 1
II. Rallies. 8
III. The Road to Panama. 13
IV. Reflections. 54
V. Alaska. 69
VI. El Camino Real. 91
VII. Tunisian Adventure 102
VIII. Favorite Roads 116
IX. Clubs and Associations 132
X. Advice 143
Dedication. 151
Bibliography. 153

Prologue

Most owners of boats, airplanes, or motorcycles christen them with pet names. I have owned a succession of five motorcycles and each bike was called "Tinker," a name I plucked out of Irish life and culture. Tinker is the title bestowed upon the itinerants of Ireland, the "traveling people." These people, similar to European Gypsies, traveled the roads of Ireland doing odd jobs such as pot and kettle repairs[1], begging, and occasionally "borrowing" a horse or two. Efforts to educate the children and settle the parents were successful only during the bad-weather months; good weather meant "on the road again." They usually traveled in their colorful, covered wagons. Today they move about in cars and trailers ("caravans"). Thus, the Tinkers are the Irish gypsies.

The word *gypsy*, incidentally, is a corruption of "Egyptian": Gypsies liked to think that their ancestral home was Egypt. Actually they originated in northwestern India. They had been one of the nomadic tribes of that region and for many years had never gone beyond its borders. About the year AD 1000 they

---

1 Tinker's dam—a very small layer of solder placed around the defect in the pot or pan to be repaired. It prevented the repair solder from flowing out of the repair area. Thus the expression, "I don't give a tinker's dam(n)."

ventured west through Persia, and on into the Byzantine Empire. By AD 1300, they were in the Balkans and Hungary. Some settled as serfs, while others were given permits to wander. These wanderers became tinkers, wood-carvers, and minstrels. Since they were shunned by many and often inhumanely treated by the police, of necessity, they developed a shrewdness in dealing with others. Some indulged in thievery of varying degrees. Yet their skills, musical and otherwise, were sought after. They usually adopted the religion of the land they traveled. The Tinkers of Ireland, some used to think, were a spin-off from these early tribes, whom they resemble in lifestyle. And this, a very verbose explanation of why my bikes were named "Tinker."

Many years before Tinker, I had ridden borrowed bikes, falling off my first ride, an *Indian* make, in 1938. During the gas-shortage days of the pre-WWII years I rode Harleys, again the borrowed type.

So now you know that "Tinker" is a motorcycle, not just any motorcycle but my own precious vehicle. Since Tinker was the moniker (a word we get from the jargon of the Irish Travelers, stonemasons, etc.) for all my bikes, it grew from a relatively light, but fast, Kawasaki to a two-stroke, 500cc Suzuki. I didn't care for the whine of a two-stroke, so after thirty-thousand miles, I traded for a 750cc Honda, a real workhorse, that carried me more than sixty thousand miles. After my trip to Panama, I felt this Tinker, battered and bruised, was entitled to retirement, so I traded for Honda's first venture into the 1000cc class, the Gold Wing. This bike featured a driveshaft, as opposed to the conventional chain drive. After a number of cross-country excursions and a run up the Alcan Highway to Alaska, I put my beaten-up Gold Wing to rest. The next Tinker was an R-100 BMW. This 1000cc touring bike, I always felt, was one of the ugliest-looking bikes, but then beauty is in the eye of the beholder. Ugly or not, this shaft-driven BMW was, without doubt, one of the most sturdy and dependable bikes ever made. And so, after 80,000 miles plus, with Mother

Nature attacking from the left and Father Time attacking from the right, and year number eighty staring me straight in the face, and at the behest of my wife and four sons, I tearfully parted with Tinker Five.

My prewar biking consisted of short rides confined to New Jersey, as mentioned, on borrowed bikes. But with the arrival of my first Tinker I became more seriously involved in the sport. While I lay no claim to the world's longest-distance rider, in subsequent years my Tinkers did carry me approximately one quarter million miles over the concrete ribbons of the interstates, the backcountry blacktops, the dirt and gravel of the Alcan, the narrow Pan-American. Tinker, I should say *Tinkers*, carried me to all our great states except Hawaii, but including Alaska, eight provinces and the Yukon Territory of Canada, and twelve countries scattered over several continents (North and Central America, Europe, and North Africa).

Together, Tinker and I, we won the Road Rider Magazine[2] "Long Distance Rider" award on two different occasions and, in 1982, won the "National Average Rider" title with a 14K year. Locally, we won the "Example Rider" award, presented by the North Haledon (N.J.) Mountaineers Motorcycle Club. I still haven't figured out what that one meant. Even so, I treasure that award more than any of the others, probably because it came from fellow bikers of my hometown. In my cross-country trips (about ten), I enjoyed visiting most of this country's national parks, but most of all, I enjoyed the visits with friends and former St. Louis University classmates sprinkled around the United States.

So much for Tinker, but who was the guy who steered him all those miles? Well, it all started when one John McCloskey met and married a certain Mary Hepworth—he from Belfast, in Ireland, and she from Dublin, Ireland (Britain aside, in my family there is only one Ireland). This union produced five offspring, three

2   Road Rider Magazine is a national publication dedicated to all motorcycle enthusiasts.

boys and two girls, with me, Joseph, in the middle. My first peek at daylight occurred on June 13, 1918 and my early years were spent as a shy, skinny kid who learned to darn his own socks and put cardboard pieces in worn-out shoes during the Depression (I refuse to call it "Great"). I was guided through grade and high school by the good Sisters of Charity, the very same nuns who invented "discipline." While struggling through high school, I managed to make the football team and still deliver newspapers at six a.m. every morning, three p.m. after school, and Sunday mornings. Finally, in 1936, I and a bunch of eager beavers were turned loose from high school with not too much to look forward to. Since I was in a hurry to set the world on fire and earn a million dollars pronto, I enrolled in the evening schedule at a state teachers college and worked days, for the grandiose salary of twelve dollars per week. As the country crept slowly out of the Depression, the dark clouds of WWII loomed ahead: Kind of like somebody blew out the light at the end of the tunnel. With a bleak future staring me, and all other young adults, in the face, I quit school and with a fellow frustrated youth, built a penny-pitch stand and headed off with a traveling carnival. The Schuylkill County Fairgrounds, Pennsylvania, was my home for the next ten days. I wouldn't attempt to describe my loving parents' concern for my sanity. They must have reasoned, "He's too dumb to teach, so let him learn on his own." And this I did. Very quickly I learned that this old world is not all on the level. My short life as a "carnie" could fill a book, and for too long my moniker became Carnie Joe. Toward the end of my Schuylkill County enterprise, England and Hitler's Germany went to war. Now my future was in the hands of others. That great philosopher who stated, "Things always look darkest just before they go pitch black," hit the nail right on the head.

My partner and I headed home for more schooling, this time machine-shop training. This resulted in a job as a gear-cutter in an airplane-engine factory. (Gears, teeth, etc. A portent of my future?)

Of course, since high school, I had become increasingly aware of girls. About this time, I also lost my shyness and, after discovering the joys of the sudsy stuff, I quickly lost my skinniness. In the year 1942, I married and continued to cut gears until Uncle Sam decided he needed me.

With my younger brother, Pat, and a few hundred other sad sacks, we found ourselves in Fort Dix, N.J. That was the last I would see my brother for three years, of course, and likewise for my older brother, John, who already had two years of the military under his belt

After one year of tramping up and down the East Coast, the Army decided we were having too much fun and doing too little for the war effort, so we were rewarded with a cruise aboard the fourth largest ship afloat. The *Mauretania* was designed to carry approximately fifteen hundred well-heeled passengers, but this trip was slightly over- booked as we cruised to merry old England with twelve thousand not so well-heeled troops aboard. After a few weeks of blacked-out Southampton, England, we crossed the Channel and soon found ourselves rope-climbing down the side of a troopship to a landing craft, and then a walk through the water to the beach near Le Havre, France. Of course D-Day was in the past, so this was more annoying than dangerous. As a replacement, I was shuffled through France and Belgium, just in time to miss the Battle of the Bulge. On to Holland, and finally I was assigned to an armored division and completed my journey through Germany as far as Berlin. No hero was I, always there just after it happened or had left just before it did. Our division (2nd Armored) had the honor of being the first American division to enter Berlin. Of course, the Russians had obtained the "first looting rights." After leaving battered Berlin (and since the war was over), I drank my way through bombed-out Frankfurt and a few smaller towns, which were equally bombed out. The good news was that I captured a furlough to England, found my way to Scotland, and crossed the sea to Belfast, Ireland. Here I looked up my relatives, who, incidentally, operated a welcome tavern. With the help of a young cousin and against all rules, I traveled to County Leitrim, Éire, to spend Christmas of the year 1945 with more of my relatives. When I returned to my unit in Germany, two weeks late, I discovered I was slated for return to the US and discharge.

The agonizingly slow sail home was soon forgotten as I celebrated a joyous reunion with my wife and family. I also carried home a more serious and mature outlook on life. Finally convinced that I couldn't drink the barrel dry, I returned to school full-time and worked part-time. With my prewar college included, I accumulated three years of predental studies, which qualified me for the St. Louis University dental program.

Four years hence, my patient wife and I returned to New Jersey, armed with my DDS and two male toddlers. While developing a dental practice, our brood was increased to four, all boys. And then, after all had completed their basic schooling, I returned to motorcycling and the story that follows.

Please keep in mind that all the biking experiences related herein occurred between the years 1965 and 1995.

I.
Maritime
Provinces

Most kids dream of growing up to become firemen, doctors, garbage men, lawyers, or president of the United States. My dream was to roam our great country by freight train, "riding the rods," as the hoboes called it. When I related this desire to my shocked mother, she passed the info to my slightly stern father. After a six-second, one-sided discussion with Dad, my dream was shattered. But I never lost the desire to wander unfamiliar lands— even after the all-expense paid tour of eight European countries, courtesy of the U.S. Army, during WWII.

As I grew older and more independent, I decided touring via motorcycle would quell my desires.

Having fallen off my first motorcycle in 1938 and ridden borrowed bikes till Uncle Sam called me to service in 1943, I felt very comfortable and completely at ease aboard two-wheelers. At this time (1974) I was on my third bike (named "Tinker," of course), and anxious to tackle my first overnight excursion.

For my maiden voyage I planned (*mis*planned would be more accurate) a relatively short trip. My itinerary called for a four-day vacation through three of the Maritime Provinces of

Canada: Nova Scotia, Prince Edward Island, and New Brunswick. Sometimes I hear people refer to Nova Scotia ("New Scotland") as an island, which is not true. It is connected to New Brunswick by a narrow isthmus. This short excursion proved to be a wise move as I learned so much from my mistakes and haphazard planning, valuable lessons that made future trips much more enjoyable.

That Friday morning, bright and early, I should have been on the road, but no, there I was in my garage, gathering and replacing Tinker's clutch plates, Tinker being a 750cc Honda. It was actually two o'clock p.m. when I was finally able to take off.

Now I knew there was a ferry service from Bar Harbor, Maine, and also one from Portland, both connecting to Yarmouth, Nova Scotia, but I hadn't bothered to check the schedules. Call that Mistake Numero Uno. Somewhere in Massachusetts I stopped for dinner, and after ordering, asked the waitress if she could find me a ferry schedule. The young lady informed me that she didn't have one, but she did know that a ferry left Portland each evening at nine p.m. and docked in Yarmouth at seven a.m. She also informed me that, since it was over sixty miles distant and it was now almost eight p.m., I wouldn't be able to make it. Well, I canceled my order and took off, rode much too fast in the darkness, and with directions provided by an I-95 toll collector, I found the ferry terminal by pure luck. Once again, poor planning and poor judgment. At the gate booth, the attendant radioed to the loader to hold for one more. Then, with Tinker securely roped to a truck onboard, I was ready to sail.

Since this was an overnight trip, and me badly in need of sleep, I put my name on standby for a cabin. After a short wait I was paged and offered a double cabin if I was willing to share with an elderly gent. He was a resident of Pennsylvania and was returning to Nova Scotia for a visit to his native land. This turned out to be a good deal for me, as I now had a bed to sleep in and my cabin mate filled me in on the history and attractions of this province. He was overflowing with interesting nuggets from the history and lore of the land, but I was just too tired to take notes, and thus much was lost to my tired mind. I skipped dinner and the temptation of the onboard casino in lieu of some much needed sleep, and a good sleep I had. Early morning, as the ship slowly entered the Bay of Fundy, I was able to observe the watermarks on the rocky cliffs, offering evidence of the very high tides. Up to 70 feet, they are possibly the highest tides in the world.

The seacoast of Nova Scotia is dotted with many villages, all replete with legends of pirates, shipwrecks, buried treasure, and of course ghosts, such as Captain Kidd. One tale related by my cabin mate tutor concerned the brig *Mary Celeste*. On a voyage out of New York in 1872, it was found adrift in the Atlantic with no crew. And I can't remember the ending to that tale, if there is one.

After debarking the ferry at Yarmouth, a port city on the southern end of Nova Scotia, I headed northeast on good blacktop to Liverpool, a fishing village at the mouth of the Mersey River, about 70 miles south of Halifax. I rested Tinker in a parking area and proceeded to survey the river edge, where I gabbed with a couple of youngsters fishing the river, and admired their catch. I guessed they would go home to a fresh fish dinner, but they informed me that, since the river was polluted, they would feed the catch to their cat. Poor cat. Shortly after, while conversing with a couple who were vacationing in their RV, they invited me to join them for a fish dinner in their camper. With the young fellows' tale of pollution fresh in mind I turned down their friendly offer, saddled up Tinker, and took off toward Peggy's Cove.

Peggy's Cove, is a must on the tourist trail. Just south of Halifax on St. Margaret's Bay the scenic beauty of this cove is made to order for artists and photographers, and many there were, sketching, painting, and shooting photos of all aspects of the scene. I also took some pictures, and while duly impressed by the cove's beauty, I was forced to move on as *tempus fugit*, et cetera.

A short jaunt north found me entering the capital city of Nova Scotia, Halifax. This busy city was the major naval base for Canada during WWI and WWII. In 1917 a munitions ship explosion killed 2,000 people and ruined the northern section of the city. (This was part of the lore imparted to me by the old timer with whom I shared the cabin.) Because of the heavy traffic, my visit to Halifax was in-and-out, and on to Sidney.

Sidney is a busy town of various industries, more or less the center of activity for Cape Breton Island. Since the shadows were growing longer, I quickened my pace. I wanted to make Prince Edward Island before darkness. Once again my inadequate planning found me riding strange roads in darkness. A definite no-no in my book of safe cycling.

Of course, having bitten off more than I could chew, I was forced to forego a planned excursion over the Cabot Trail, a scenic trail circling the upper end of the island, through rugged coastal mountains. I put the Cabot Trail on my "must do" list, but alas, it now rests deep in my "never got to" list.

From Sidney I backtracked and headed for Pictou with its nearby ferry slip, and a short sail across a narrow portion of the Northumberland Strait to Prince Edward Island, hereafter called P.E.I. Near Pictou, I passed the town of Antigonish, the location of St. Ann's, the only Gaelic college in North America, and the scene of the Mòd[3] or festival, the Highland Games. Once free of the ferry, I had about fifty miles of nighttime riding to reach Charlottetown. I would have been very happy to hole up for the night, but the fifty-mile route showed me only a few small towns and if there were any motels they were well hidden.

The night ride over strange roads was made without a hitch as I followed a fast moving truck the entire route. After two

3   That's *féile*, or *feis*, for you Irish folks

"No Vacancies," I stumbled on what was probably the one and only available room in Charlottetown, a very large efficiency, fully equipped with everything I didn't need. Seems this was homecoming week for something or other, thus the shortage of rooms. From Yarmouth to Charlottetown via Halifax and Sidney is approximately 700 miles, so at this point all I needed was a shower and bed, and I promptly made good use of both. Charlottetown is the capital and largest city on P.E.I. Anything else about this city I had to look up later in the big book, as I had arrived in darkness and departed before full light.

Prince Edward Island, first colonized by the French, is the smallest province in the world's second largest country, Canada. P.E.I. and Nova Scotia were the setting for French-English battles and re-battles. Finally, England won the field and deported the settlers, and the land was awarded to landlords in England, "absentee ownership," an injustice perfected by the Brits (witness Ireland, among other places). Naturally, this impeded the island's development. The island is relatively level. Maybe rolling plains and low hills says it better. Its highest point is 465 feet above sea level.

But now back to Tinker. From the capital I circled the island and found myself at Cavendish Beach, one of the many fine, wide strands of P.E.I., but once again I could only afford a too-short visit. Although this tour through the Maritimes was relatively short in miles (approximately 1,400 miles), I just did not allow sufficient time to fully absorb the beauty of the land and, more important, the people. Completing the circle of the island led me to the small town of Borden, where I boarded the ferry for a short hop over the Northumberland Strait at its narrowest point, to Cape Tormentine. Which now puts us—Tinker and me—in the province of New Brunswick. A short, comfortable, unhurried ride over good country roads led to Moncton, and then touring in a southwesterly direction for a hundred miles, I arrived in the city of Saint John. Saint John is the largest city in

New Brunswick and sits at the mouth of the Saint John River as it empties into the Bay of Fundy. Both Moncton and Saint John experience a weird phenomenon. The sixty-mile long Petitcodiac River, at Moncton, has a tidal bore, a single river-wide wave that moves upstream daily. The height is determined by the phase of the moon. Saint John has a similar situation—the reversing falls. Strong tidal fluctuations reverse the river's flow for several miles upstream, twice each day. These strange tidal happenings are no doubt influenced by the record high tides of the Bay of Fundy. (Please note that Saint John, in New Brunswick, should not be confused with St. Johns of Newfoundland.)

From Saint John my trail led to St. Stephen, where I crossed the border back into the United States. For a change I didn't have to hurry, so I took U.S. Route 1 South from Calais, Maine, a scenic winding road, made to order for bikes. Tinker enjoyed it immensely. Near Whiting, I drifted off course to the town of Lubec, with its sign proclaiming it the "Eastermost" town in the US. Back on Route 1, I reached the town of Ellsworth, where I booked into a motel, and after the usual welcome shower and dinner, hit the sack. Early next morning, I bid Ellsworth farewell and toured that popular summer resort, Bar Harbor. Located on Mount Desert Island, it is also subjected to extremely high tides. Bar Harbor serves as headquarters for Acadia National Park, Maine's only national park. From Bar Harbor I took Rte. 3, which will take you on an exciting circular tour of Acadia Park.

This drive around the park is well worth the time and effort, and I recommend you do it by motorcycle to fully appreciate its rugged beauty. Continuing on Rte. 3, I passed Ellsworth and continued on to Belfast, to connect to US Rte. 1 South. I enjoyed that wandering road until I finally reached the town of Brunswick and reality, the boring Interstate I-95. The interstate took me to Portsmouth, New Hampshire, where I followed Route 4 to Concord, New Hampshire's capital, and a visit with a classmate from St. Louis U days. After a hasty reunion and testing the quality of New Hampshire brew, I hit the road southward. Concord to home is roughly 300 miles, and since I stuck to the interstates or other major highways it was an easy ride, even with my wind and sunburned lips and cheeks.

Within a few days after arriving at my home in North Haledon, N.J., my lips began to blister and my face started to peel. (, "Haledon," by the way, is pronounced with only two syllables: HALE-dun.) The bright sun and the wind had done their job well. Among the numerous errors I had committed was embarking on this excursion without providing Tinker with a windshield and a face shield for my helmet. Before my next encounter with the open road I resolved to install both. My next resolve was always to study a map of my intended routes, as well as any pertinent schedules, such as ferries. Also I promised myself I would read up on the land and people, the history, culture, and religion, and lastly carry all necessary equipment and spare parts that I hopefully would not need.

Finally, if you plan a visit to these interesting provinces, allow sufficient time to fully enjoy the land and the people.

II.
Rallies

As previously stated, I prefer to ride solo. But I have also participated in many "poker runs," because they were dedicated to various local charities. I also attended many annual meetings of the Motorcycling Doctors Association. These gatherings of thirty to forty members did not qualify as rallies. Large rallies were not yet the vogue, but a short news item on one rally sparked my interest. The article described the first Aspencade, which was held in Ruidoso, New Mexico. To satisfy my curiosity, I decided to attend the second session. Since I'm a loner, you might wonder why I would ride 2,000 miles to join a group of approximately twelve hundred bikers. All I can say is, it got the better of my curiosity, and it did offer an excellent excuse for another cross-country ride.

This rally was scheduled for early fall, September 1970. I started out in a southern direction. Interstate 81 provided the most convenient route until I picked up I-40 in North Carolina. Somewhere near the panhandle of Texas I took a break at a rest stop, and there I met up with a trio of old-timers from South Carolina heading for this same Aspencade. They were dressed (I should say overdressed) in true winter garb. They kindly invited me to join them for the remaining two-hundred-plus miles. After many hours of slow motion one of the trio ran out of gas. They were devastated as we were in a very desolate area. I checked the fuel supply of the other bikes and then disconnected the gas line and drew about a pint, cup by cup, from each tank, which, when added to the empty tank, was enough to reach the next service station. Now we all had sufficient energy to reach Ruidoso. Upon arrival, I bid adieu to my friendly companions and hied to my reserved room, complete with a malfunctioning air conditioner. Since it couldn't be corrected, I moved to one of the few remaining available motel rooms.

This Aspencade, with its displays, competitions, and grand parade featuring bikes, of course, and also horses, was well organized. During the parade I witnessed one horse, spooked by the noise of approximately three hundred bikes, gallop off to the hinterland with his helpless rider astride. More interesting was the meeting with two Texan brothers. Together we participated in a group ride to Lincoln Courthouse. Supposedly, or for real, the notorious Billy the Kid escaped his trial by jumping from the window of the courthouse. The ride, which consisted of approximately four hundred bikes, was well supervised by N.M. state troopers. My Texas buddies and I decided this affair was quite boring and they suggested a ride to Roswell, N.M., for a steak dinner, so off we went. After a very satisfying dinner we headed back to Ruidoso. The seventy-five-mile ride of exciting, twisting blacktop was a cycling pleasure. It easily surpassed our after-dinner dessert.

In order to take a break from the crowd, my Texas friends and I took a ride up Sierra Blanca. The road, or lack of it, winds its way up to almost the 10,000-foot level, and then a cable car, *sans* the bikes, carries you 2,000 feet higher up the mountain for a beautiful view of the surrounding countryside, smoking Indian workers included. Something about their smiles and the aromatic air led us to wonder what they were smoking.

On getaway day I bid my friends a good-bye and headed south, vowing to stay clear of all motorcycle rallies. Apparently, my aversion to crowds was not shared by many fellow bikers—witness the growing numbers and size of motorcycle gatherings. Highway 70 south led me through Las Cruces, N.M., to Interstate 10 which I followed into El Paso for a refreshing visit with another of my St. Louis U buddies and his family. A welcome night's rest, a relaxing round of golf, plenty of chit-chat, home-made tortillas, and then a reluctant farewell to my very hospitable friends.

The weather was just perfect, but the autumn chill would soon arrive as I headed north. So I took the southern route as far as possible. This dictated I-10 to I-20, until I reached I-95 in South Carolina. After a one-night layover near the North Carolina border, I steered Tinker in the direction of New Jersey. Five days of biking the interstates is not very exciting, but it did provide plenty of time to dwell on rallies and was also the quickest route home.

After settling into my work routine, I now had time to research the motorcycle rally milieu. The first item that caught my attention was an article that referred to the "Big Four." The Big Four turned out to be the Sturgis Motorcycle Rally, Laconia Motorcycle Week, Daytona Bike Week, and Myrtle Beach Bike Week. I soon learned that practically every state in the US has a rally. With the arrival of the 21st century the number of rallies reached sixty. One time, in Sturgis, South Dakota, while I was supping on my first taste of buffalo steak, I was surprised to learn that the Sturgis Rally was inaugurated in the year 1934. Since then I had always thought of Sturgis as the granddaddy of all rallies. And now after all these years, I discovered that Laconia Bike Week started in 1916, which makes it the oldest. It is held annually at Weirs Beach, Lake Winnipesaukee, in New Hampshire.

For gross numbers, I would nominate Daytona Bike Week. By the time I complete this essay, it is expected to reach 500,000 bikers in attendance. The first was held in 1937 and featured a motorcycle race over a beach road course. In 1961 the race was moved to Daytona Speedway. The "week" has grown to a ten-day event, which supports its claim to be the world's largest motorcycle rally.

The Myrtle Beach Rally started in 1940. The beautiful setting and great weather may be factors in raising the total attendance to approximately 300,000 by the year 2004.

All rallies feature competitions and/or professional races, great merchandising shows, exhibits, and demo rides. The rallies display the latest manufacturers' offerings of parts, accessories, apparel, and anything that can possibly be connected to motorcycling. Smaller rallies may offer guided bike tours of surrounding scenic areas. A description of all rallies would fill an entire book, but since my space is limited, a glance at a few will have to do.

Most, if not all, motorcycle rallies involve charities. The Harley Davidson Love Ride started as a carnival to aid the Muscular Dystrophy Association. This ride, out of Glendale, California, is one of the largest one-day rallies, with more than 20,000 participants. This nonprofit ride has raised more than $17 million for the MDA. Each year it attracts celebrities such as Peter Fonda, Jay Leno, and Willie Davidson. It provides top name entertainment, trade shows, food, stunts, and, of course, that special camaraderie of caring bikers.

Another rally that caught my eye was the Black Bike Week, which is of course primarily African-American. The affair, held at Myrtle Beach, is approaching an attendance figure of 200,000. In my biking days, I have never myself seen evidence of racial issues. One time, at a poker run in N.J., I noticed a black biker dancing in harmony with the vibrations of a Harley. I clicked his picture and took his name so I could forward a copy to him. He reciprocated by inviting me to visit to his home club. About a month later I delivered the pic and I was treated as a fellow member. If all the world would live as harmoniously as the majority of bikers, how better off we would be.

When discussing any phase of the motorcycling world, let us not forget our third-wheel comrades: trikers and sidecar adherents. Nor the rapidly increasing number of women bikers.

The Women on Wheels Rally is heading for its twentieth anniversary as I write this. For more info, log onto www.womenonwheels.org.

The Sidecar Rally is held in Griffith Park, Los Angeles, California, and is approaching its thirty-fourth annual event.

I'm now in over my head in rallies: so many, so varied, and so widespread. Similar to the motorcycle clubs and associations, most rallies are organized according to brand names, activities, and ideals. I guess I'm still a lone loner. If motorcycle rallies interest you, please log on to www.motorcycle.org. From this site, you can search for the present-year schedule.

III.
The Road to Panama

From the California gold-rush days came the expression "off to see the elephant." Men left their homes in the East and headed west in search of some highly exotic enterprise, a confrontation with things or conditions they did not know, a journey into a vast and frightening unknown. Well, some of them struck it rich, most went broke, but they all had an adventure and thus "saw the elephant." Now, I would like to take you with me as we go off to see this elephant. All my journeys began at morning Mass, not to pray for my safety or good luck, but, well, I think the following prayer says it best. This prayer was copied from an informative booklet placed in various motel rooms in western Canada by the Knights of Columbus:

"O Lord, help me to drive with a steady hand, a sure eye, and perfect control, so that I might bring no harm to others using the same roads. Thou art the Author of life. Therefore I beseech Thee, permit me not to be the cause of the death of any one of those for whom Thou hast given Thy life.

"Protect, O Lord, those who accompany me from every mishap or accident. Teach me to make use of this machine for my fellow man's welfare and to curb my desire for excessive speed.

May the beauty of this world Thou has created, together with the joy of Thy grace, ever accompany me on my travels."

And now we're off to Panama. Well not quite yet. The journey really began approximately six months before I hit the road. After perusing five books concerning the history, people, religion, customs, politics, and taboos of Central America, I was ready to apply for the necessities that would make this trek possible. This meant a visit to the consular office of each country of that region. After three visits to New York City, I had acquired the visas and permits needed to proceed. Since I lived only eighteen miles west of New York City, this was no problem.

If you plan to drive down through Central America, reconsider. If you insist, I'll briefly list the items you will need and mention a few pertinent facts:

1. A U.S. passport is necessary for ID en route and for reentry to the United States.
2. Visas are required for entry to each country, and possibly photos, vehicle insurance, and special permits to remain in any given country for more than a few days. You may obtain these permits at the local consular office, if you can find it.
3. A WHO (World Health Organization) Card is no longer needed but it's wise to learn which disease is fashionable at the time of your visit, and get the appropriate shot. Malaria was active while I was there.
4. Register your cameras and lenses with U.S. Customs before you leave. Port Newark in New Jersey was most convenient for me.
5. Select the dry season for your trip, which is usually October to May. The Caribbean coast of Central America has, in my opinion, only one season—wet.
6. Carnet—Some countries require one, especially in South America. It means you must deposit a sum equal to, or more

than, the value of your vehicle. If you attempt to depart said country *sans* your vehicle, you forfeit your carnet.

And now for a few don'ts. Don't sleep on the ground in a bedroll as you may have the company of land crabs or ticks seeking warmth. Use a hammock. Don't travel the roads at night as you might encounter a variety of animals seeking the warmth of the macadam. Don't carry drugs or weapons. Film and liquor are permitted in specified amounts. If you do have any excess, spread them throughout your luggage. I carried twenty rolls of film (ten was legit) and two packs of CaOH to keep the film moisture-free. I also mailed exposed film directly to Kodak as soon as possible. The Kodak Company is, or was, cleared to process film and censor it for customs. Finally, don't discuss politics or religion, and it helps to compliment the natives on their beautiful weather, even if it's raining.

My travel kit included the usual tools: spare tube, (tubeless tires were not yet the vogue for motorcycles), patch kit, hand pump, spray oil for drive-chain maintenance, a pre-addressed bag to mail my cold weather gear home, and pre-addressed postcards which I mailed every second or third day. If I disappeared, folks would know the approximate area of my disappearance. I also tucked away $200 in my zippered belt to be used for bus fare in case Tinker pooped out, and a letter of credit against my home bank account in case I needed funds (which I did). My patient wife was aware of these measures and knew to expect regular phone calls, about every third day or whenever I happened to be in a city. Small villages just didn't have the technology for such calls in 1975. Originally I had planned to ride to Miami, Florida, board a ferry (the same one used for summer service on the Maine-to-Nova Scotia route that I had previously taken), and sail to Mérida or Puerta Morelos on the Yucatan peninsula of Mexico. This plan was frustrated by the cancellation of the ferry service.

After a farewell party given by my large and raucous family it was necessary to delay my departure by one day. Finally, I was ready to begin the first leg of the trek: a two- thousand mile ride from North Jersey to the border of Mexico. On April 11, 1975, I headed west on Route 80, but due to slippery road conditions I had to hole up near Pittsburgh. The balance of the ride to Texas was uneventful, with just a little rain and patchy fog. At Harlingen, Texas, I mailed the pre-addressed package containing my cold-weather gear back to Jersey and headed for the border. Crossed the Rio Grande from Brownsville to Matamoros for fifteen cents. The reverse crossing cost six cents. Border towns and seaports, I have found, are usually wild and scary. Maybe not dangerous, but definitely unsafe. Now if that statement confuses you, you're with me. My first move in Mexico was to hire a taxi driver to escort me to customs and then to lead me to the Pan-American Highway. Why a taxi? Matamoros was a mass of bedlam and confusion, and for $1.65 the taxi driver was my best buy of the year. Since Mexico considers herself part of North America, there is still approximately 1,200 miles before reaching Central America. At the Mexican customs station, the agent informed me that my papers were not in order, but he could correct them for $8 dollars. With the help of the taxi driver, we negotiated and I paid two dollars *mordida* (bribe). Next, a young coyote (go-fer) was sent with me to make sure my license number was the same as that on the paperwork. The young lad shyly requested his "teep," and the twenty-five cents I gave him brought forth the happiest face I'd seen in a long time. All this after three trips to the Mexican consulate in New York. But my pre-trip studies had prepared me well for all present and future border hassles. Now the taxi, Tinker, and I traveled exactly one mile to a police checkpoint and then, after about twenty-five miles, a military checkpoint. Since most Mexicans like *motos* (motorcycles), I encountered no problems. The *mordida*, or "bite," is a way of life south of the border, so get used to it and try to keep your sanity.

My helpful taxi driver waved a good-bye at Highway 101 after refusing any additional money for all his extra efforts. He was the first example of what I found repeatedly as the trip progressed, that almost all the people I met on this trip were kind, honest, and helpful. It seems the less the people have, the more honest they are.

Highway 101 led me to Victoria. Gas stations are few and far between, and offer a wide selection—Pemex or Pemex. That's the government's brand of gas. En route to Victoria the scenery is flat and scrubby with all kinds of things on the road: people, donkeys, goats, cows, occasionally some cars and trucks, and roadside pyramids of oranges patiently waiting for some rickety truck to carry them to market. Two-lane roads in Mexico are barely that, "oversized one-lane" would describe them better. I would guess that these roads and bridges had been designed for horse and carriage rather than today's vehicles, and so, as you approach a bridge and an oncoming truck blinks its lights, it means that the driver is claiming the right of way. Since there is room for only one, yield. Don't argue with trucks. Along the road, the donkeys appear strong and the cows sickly, and around the villages are too many stray dogs. Found Victoria about noon and after a Coke and an undersized turnover I headed for Ciudad Valles. I crossed the Tropic of Cancer south of Victoria (the exciting event of the day), and finally the flat terrain gave way to scenic mountains with tricky curves and bumps in the road. The lack of warning signs and guardrails makes for very cautious driving. The mountains become even more beautiful as you climb to 6,000 feet. From Valles to Mexico City is only about 250 kilometers. But because of the tricky roads, it's almost an all-day journey. Finally I reached the inevitable toll road that led me into the city. Five p.m. is not the ideal time to enter Mexico City. I rode along Insurgentes Norte which, for more confusion, connected to the Paseo de la Reforma. This broad, tree-lined avenue leading to Chapultepec ("grasshopper") Park, planned by

Emperor Maximillian to resemble the Champs Elysées in Paris. A beautiful boulevard—avoid it. After an hour of stop-and-go, I found a Pemex station and a taxi driver who led me to a nice new motel on the outskirts of the confusion. This was my base for two days of guided tours.

After a good night's rest, I taxied to the Hotel Continental in the *centro* of Mexico City and signed on for a morning bus tour of the city. This tour is guaranteed to show you all the desirable aspects of the city, including Chapultepec Park and the surrounding luxury homes. Since I had signed on for an afternoon private tour of the pyramids, I decided to have lunch at the same hotel. While enjoying an exquisite lunch, I was shocked to hear my name being paged a la "Johnny" from the Phillip Morris days ("Call for Phillip Morris!" circa 1939). Gingerly, I answered the call and found, to my surprise, that a representative of the tour bus company had found $500 of my traveler's checks while cleaning the bus. He positively refused a reward for himself or the driver and begged off my offer to share lunch. Beautiful, honest people, I love them and couldn't feel more at home. While waiting for the afternoon tour to materialize, I discovered a few interesting facts regarding this very busy city. Mexico City, the focal point of a land of contrasts, land of the Aztecs, Toltecs, Zapotecs, and VWs, rests at 7,000 feet above sea level. It is the center of Mexico's industry, culture, and education; it is the oldest city in North America, a continuation of the Aztec capital, Tenochtitlán, founded about AD 1325. The city is built over several lakes and the supply of water is decreasing, so the city is literally sinking. Since the year 1920, the city has sunk approximately twenty feet.

The afternoon tour consisted of a driver, a not-so-new van, a couple from New Jersey, and myself. We headed out of the city to visit the pyramids. It's only about twenty-five miles to Teotihuacán, the location of the Pyramids of the Sun and Moon, plus numerous other structures. The Pyramid of the Sun is the higher one, but I climbed the Pyramid of the Moon, because its location at the periphery of the area provided an ideal spot to photograph just about the entire site. The pyramids and surrounding structures are a grand sight, and definitely worthy of a visit. On the return trip our driver explained why pairs of motorcycle cops would sit at traffic lights and periodically ticket cars for supposedly running the light. Tickets cost enough pesos to equal about $1.50 and are payable in cash. Like *now*. Complaints are few and the *mordida* does help augment the officer's meager salary. After a visit to the Plaza of Three Cultures, which is a small area containing buildings by Aztec, Spanish, and modern architects, we continued on to visit the shrine of the Virgin of Guadalupe and University City, with its famous murals. An interesting sidelight to our visit at the shrine of Guadalupe was the sight of several women moving slowly on their knees for hundreds of yards until they reached the shrine. This is part of a ritual performed as an offering or a sacrifice as they seek resolution of some problem or an answer to an urgent need. To ease the discomfort, another person, usually the husband, spreads a towel or blanket in her path. As she progresses, he retrieves the towel and again places it in her path. I couldn't help but imagine some of these women might very well be seeking a divine answer to said hubby's drinking or other problem. I was told quite often that Central American Indians don't hold the booze too well, and exhibit abusive actions toward their family while under the influence. Maybe not too different from other poor and rather oppressed people in the world. Our tour's final attraction was a visit to the Palacio Nacional, located in the Zócalo[4]. Here we viewed the murals of Diego Rivera, probably Mexico's most renowned artist. At the top of the main staircase at the *palacio* is his depiction of his vision of postrevolutionary Mexico. On the second floor, we viewed many more examples of Rivera's talent. While I am definitely not a connoisseur of the arts, I couldn't help but be overwhelmed by this man's artistry.

4   *Zócalo* means" town" or "city square."

Early the following morning I rode south about forty miles to catch a glimpse of snowcapped Popocatepetl and Iztaccihuatl, two dormant volcanoes, rising more than 17,000 feet.

Now on to my next stop, Oaxaca, a beautiful city nestled in a deep, quiet valley, with enough attractions to warrant a three-day layover. En route to Oaxaca, while enjoying some liquid refreshment, I met a fellow biker, from Colorado. He was on his way to Nicaragua to dust crops. At fifty cents per acre, this would add up to approximately $800 per week. After quaffing a cool Corona *cerveza* we rode on to Oaxaca. We booked into the same motel, and while relaxing later at the bar, our conversation was interrupted by a loud crash. We rushed out to the darkened road and found a young lad and his girlfriend lying on the road. After helping them to a safe spot, we moved their small motorcycle away from further danger. The young fellow definitely suffered a broken jaw and possibly a broken arm; his companion, although quite shaken, was unhurt. An obvious case of hit-and-run, which is all too common in Mexico. People don't stop because the police have a habit of keeping all those involved in the hoosegow (from the Spanish *juzgado*), including any available witnesses, until the law feels ready to dispose of the case. For this reason we had the motel clerk call for help, while we got lost.

Next morning my aviator friend headed south, and I rode up the mountain to visit Monte Albán. This site was built about AD 500 and contains carvings, temples, steles, and courts. The courts were used to play forms of jai alai and basketball, which they played for keeps, since the losing captain literally lost his head, presented to the leader of the winners. Not very far from Monte Albán is Mitla, a small area of ancient structures. I was told this was a Zapotec Indian burial ground. Later, after evening Mass at Santo Domingo Church, with its beautiful, ornately decorated altar, I met an elderly American couple traveling from Panama to Florida. They were driving a VW van with their pet dog, and after discussing our border hassles we went our separate ways. While having dinner, I met another American, a nice black woman from Maryland, whose husband had retired, and since the beautiful weather in the Oaxaca valley suited his ailing health, they planned to move there. She didn't speak Spanish so she asked me to make a selection from the greasy menu. I suggested *pollo frito*, because those two words used up my entire Spanish food vocabulary. She was duly impressed.

Arbol de Tule ("tree of Tule") was the next attraction before leaving Oaxaca, one of my favorite cities. The tree, touted as the oldest tree in the world, is thought to be at least 3,000 years old, has a perimeter of 175 feet, and a height of 150 feet. As you can imagine, any plant this size needs plenty of water, so an underground watering system was constructed to keep the tree alive.

The drive south toward the Guatemalan border was not bad until I hit the semi-desert area, where I experienced a flat tire on the rear wheel. At seventy mph, a scary situation. With a can of tire-repair fluid and a hand pump as part of my arsenal, I felt quite secure but the high heat build-up caused too big a rip in the tube for any makeshift measure. Now I had to dig out my spare tube, remove the wheel, and replace the blown tube. Not a major task, but in the hot sun, with no available shade, it turned into a two-hour drag. Of course, removing the tire with two six-inch tire irons didn't make the task any easier. With the job just about completed, except for adjusting the chain, along came the only vehicle I had seen in more than two hours, a Green Angel. The Mexican government provides a great road service that covers the Pan-American Highway twice each day. Small green trucks, driven by young mechanics, offering aid and supplies to stranded motorists, are nicknamed "the Green Angels," and that they are. This particular young fellow insisted on completing my task, even though I had to tell him how to do it. The service is free but they will accept a tip, which they truly deserve.

Tuxtla Gutiérrez, the capital city of the state of Chiapas, lies about one hundred miles south of my flat tire and there I found, if you stretch your imagination a little, a luxury hotel. You don't get a key to your room, but the porter opens the door each time you return to your room. Before leaving Tuxtla I attempted to purchase a new tube to carry as a spare, but they wouldn't hear of it. Instead, they re-vulcanized the old one for thirty-five cents.

The hundred miles remaining to the border proved to be very scenic, interrupted only by the last *aduana* in Mexico. Here my papers were checked again, and I received a stamped paper allowing me to proceed, only to have it retrieved by a gate officer a few hundred yards down the road. There is a nice level route along the coast from Tuxtla to Guatemala, but I chose the more scenic Route 190. This route leads you through the towering, rugged mountains and through the pass called el Tapón ("the plug"). I encountered one mountain slide, and to prevent you from driving into the abyss, large boulders, painted yellow, were placed across the road and then a ledge was bulldozed out of the mountainside. The scenery is awesome and the extra effort is well worth it. If you ride down, I highly recommend el Tapón.

In Mexico, military checkpoints pop up unexpectedly, and I flew by the final one, but quickly hit the brakes and returned to a smiling guard holding an antiquated rifle. After checking my papers we had a long chat regarding motorcycles and the local area. He insisted I visit Lake Comitán and, like a good tourist, I did. I felt he was a little disappointed that I had stopped and thus denied him some good old-fashioned target practice. Moral of the story, "never pass a checkpoint of any kind."

At the Guatemalan aduana, my visa and passport were checked in slow motion and I was issued a license for Tinker, a metal ring sealed to the bike. This was followed by a spray job for my tires. I was told this is a preventive medicine measure. As usual you keep quiet and pay the nominal fee of one quetzal for each bit of official rigamarole, a quetzal being equal to one dollar. Each

Central American country naturally has its own currency with varying exchange rates to the dollar. *Time* magazine conveniently displays the currency of each country with its current rate of exchange on the front cover. I kept one front cover so I could keep abreast of my daily finances. A very helpful item, especially when you're in each country for only a few days.

Once clear of customs, police, and military checkpoints, we are now in Central America. Central America, or C. A., has a population of about 25 million people—mestizos, of mixed white and Indian heritage, make up half the population. Indians, make up 20 percent and are concentrated in Guatemala and Nicaragua. Whites are dominant in Costa Rica, and blacks and mulattos in Panama and the Caribbean coastal plains of all the countries. In 1492, Mexico, Central America, and South America had approximately 70 million people. Within 50 years after the arrival of the Spaniards more than half the Indians had perished. Within a century only 25% remained. Why? The Spaniards were brutal and cruel, but most died because of the introduction of European diseases such as smallpox and measles. The Indians had no natural immunity to these conditions.

But now back to Tinker, who is anxiously waiting to hit the road. I rode the very scenic highway, excuse me, scenic trail, to Huehuetenango (way-way-teh-NAN-go). This town was well off the tourist route, which makes it even more beautiful. From my pre-trip studies, I had learned about the Hotel Zaculeu. It sounded quaint, so I located it and booked in. The only lock on my tiny room was a screen door latch. I had been warned that the rooms of strangers are often officially checked while they are absent, and I know mine was, since my notes were in a slightly different spot than where I had left them. An excellent reason not to carry contraband or get involved politically. At the time of my visit to Guatemala, 2,000 people were, well, just disappearing each year. One more good reason to keep my family aware of my approximate location at all times. Reports and statistics from later years proved this to be true, not only for 1975, but also for approximately ten other years. Add to this the 35,000 killed by earthquakes and hurricanes in Guatemala and Nicaragua since 1970.

After a hot shower (minus the "hot"), I headed for the fanciest hotel in town for dinner and it turned out to be a pleasant pension, or upgraded rooming-house. My meal consisted of beef, beans, tortilla, cookies, plantains, and coffee, all for seventy-five cents U.S. While finishing my coffee and catching up on my notes, the lights flickered and, then, there was darkness. Very quickly the candles were lighted. And I had thought the candles were for atmosphere. Many small towns are able to generate electricity for only a limited number of hours each day. Back in my $1.75 cubicle, my small flashlight came in handy.

Motorcycles can be very easily lifted to a truck by any two dedicated thieves, so if you are traveling by bike I recommend you choose only those inns that provide secured courtyards or other protection. Following this procedure I was ensured a good night's sleep. I did meet one gent who lost some goodies from his locked car, but what confused him was the fact that the car was again locked when he discovered his loss.

As the guard opened the gate to allow my departure I noticed my saddlebags didn't look quite kosher. A quick inspection disclosed a bilateral fracture of Tinker's rear support frame, probably due to the constant pounding from the rough roads. An English-speaking Texaco dealer (once free of Mexico you are actually offered a small choice of petrol dealers) directed me to a native Indian welder. Very gingerly, I followed the rocky dirt trail up the side of a nearby mountain and found father, son, and German shepherd, all friendly, but their welding machine was out of commission. After one-and-a-half hours of cleaning and adjusting the carburetor, I had it running and, with the seat, gas tank, and saddlebags removed, he proceeded to complete a crude but very effective weld. Two years and over 5,000 miles later, when I sold Tinker, the weld was still solid. Ready to leave, I asked "Quánto?" He answered with his face a question mark. I offered U.S. $20, knowing it was worth at least $30, but he indicated "too much." With our best mutual sign language he refused $10 and suggested $5. I finally convinced him to accept five for himself and five for his very helpful son, and zero for the German shepherd who contributed nothing but an evil eye. Once again honest, admirable people, and I departed amid feelings of guilt.

About noon, I kissed Huehuetenango a reluctant good-bye but not before I stopped at a small shop to say so-long to the beautiful black couple from the Chicago area who operated their little outlet in this quaint town. Their conversations gave me much comfort and joy during my short stay there. Surprising how Americans wind up staying in isolated places like this.

As you wander about the villages and towns of Guatemala, you will, no doubt, become aware of Cristo Negro, the Black Christ. The Black Christ is represented by a statue carved out of dark wood. It was fashioned about 200 years ago. Cristo Negro has generated a faith of great depth and magnitude, not only in the Indians of Guatemala but throughout Central America. If proof be needed, witness the two pilgrimages each year to Esquipulas to pay homage to this figure. One occurs in January and the second during Easter Week. Indians—and many non-Indians—travel for weeks to complete the pilgrimage. Sadly, all my inquiries left me totally confused regarding the whole situation, mainly due to my lack of Spanish. I have witnessed feast days where the Indians came to honor their patron saint and then park their idols or relics of a former belief outside the church. Kind of like covering all the bases. With Cristo Negro I firmly believe the natives were fully dedicated to Jesus Christ.

You can bet the ride from Huehuetenango to Solola was a very cautious one since my confidence in the weld job was still a bit shaky. Sometimes a nice sunny day is spoiled by a black cloud and this particular bright day's dark cloud came in the form of a solemn procession of nine local people. The small group was led by four men shouldering a plain wooden casket as they plodded on to the burial ground. The size of the box left no doubt that it held the remains of a small child. As I passed this tragic scene and glanced back, I was tempted to snap a photo, but not wishing to intrude on this family's time of sorrow, I offered a quiet prayer and moved on.

In Solola, Tinker was thirsty so I filled the tank at a local excuse for a service station. The operator would have no part of my Yankee dollars or American Express card, and me without quetzals. Plus I was unaware that he had latched onto my ignition key. To resolve the dilemma, he directed his son and me (without Tinker) to a local bank, about a quarter mile distance, where I converted dollars to quetzals. Luckily we hit the bank minutes before closing. Another lesson—make sure you have enough local currency to survive without credit cards. My American Express card was rejected too many times in out-of-the-way places to make it worthwhile. I discarded it, along with my dirty socks. From Solola, a dirt road took me around Lake Atitlán, to San Lucas Tolimán. Lake Atitlán is billed as the most beautiful lake in the world, and I must agree that it is. Here you see grass-roofed huts, bare feet, skirts bearing the patterns of various Indian families, and women carrying jugs of water, among other things, on their heads. The lake is surrounded by hopefully extinct volcanoes. A very impressive sight. In the village I visited the small mission of Father Gregory Schaeffer, hailing from Minnesota, USA. Father established a mission, followed by a small medical and dental clinic. The infant mortality rate in San Lucas Talimán was 60% in 1975, and the midwife's fee for delivering a girl was three quetzals, for a boy five. As I snapped photos of the mission and clinic, I chatted with the young dentist and his helpers. Father Gregory was away, so I missed the pleasure of meeting him. Day by day, my feelings for these people grew stronger, and thus it was with saddened heart that I rode off toward Antigua, the old capital of Guatemala (actually its third).

For the exorbitant fee of 19 quetzals ($19), I found the fanciest setup thus far: swimming pool, garden, porch off each room, and the usual enclosed parking area. Signing the registration was like writing my biography: where I was going, where I had been, name, address, passport number, and occupation. A few times I named my address as 1600 Pennsylvania Avenue, Washington, D.C., just to see if they would notice. They did not. After a warm shower, I enjoyed a welcome martini as the waiter delivered my own complimentary drink. He even forced a second martini on me. My flat tire in the desert and cracked frame experience made this luxurious treatment all the more exotic. So far, I had eaten native foods with no sign of "turista," so my supply of Lomotil[5] remained intact. Since I was living in such upscale style, the next morning I hired a taxi to tour the results of the 1773 earthquake. Good choice, since the cobblestone streets would be rather hard on my mended Tinker, and the cabby, like most cabbies down here, really knew the local history. The complete half-day tour cost $3.

Antigua, formerly Santiago de los Caballeros, was a great city in its day but suffered too many disasters. The earthquake and floods of 1773 totally destroyed the city, which had boasted thirty churches, eighteen convents, fifteen monasteries, a university, seven colleges, five hospitals, and one orphanage. Most of the dramatic ruins have been left untouched—a photographer's dream. Quite obvious why they moved the capital to a safer place, if there is such a spot in Central America. The Arch of Catarina is an intriguing attraction. It provided passage from the convent to the church across the street. The clock in the center of the arch supposedly has wooden works.

Guatemala City, the present capital, is only seventy-five miles distant and I arrived about noon. Booked into the Hotel

5   A small white pill used to combat diarrhea.

Centenario, not the best, maybe a few steps above the fleabag class, but the price was right and the shower water was warm. It also had a safe haven for Tinker and was located right off the main plaza, very handy to buses and cabs. The city is served by wide streets for the most part, and even sports a small version of the Eiffel Tower, a gift from somebody to somebody for something. Stumbled onto the phone company, so I sat in my assigned booth while the operator connected me to home, a very efficient service, but only available in major cities. My next chore was to visit the El Salvador consul's office to try and ease my entry to that country, no easy task as the office moved frequently. Now, with a free afternoon on my hands, I took a six-cent bus ride to the end of the line, and viewed the great concrete relief map of Guatemala in Minerva Park. You must view it from a raised platform, as it covers more than half an acre. If you are pressed for time, skip it. Well, skip it anyway. Next morning, six a.m. found me boarding a very doubtful looking DC-3 for a two-hundred-mile flight to the ancient Mayan city of Tikal. After a relatively smooth flight, we landed on a strip of machete-cleared runway, little more than the width of the plane, and like most of the roads in Guatemala, very bumpy. I have learned that the airstrip has been improved and is now one-mile long. I heartily recommend you try this side trip.

Tikal is a story too complex and lengthy to describe here. Briefly, Tikal lies at the southern end of the Yucatan Peninsula, in the jungles of Petén (the northern third of Guatemala). This and other Mayan cities compared favorably to European ones in culture and administrative acumen. For some unknown reason the Mayan empire suddenly collapsed and disappeared—many theories why, but few facts. The "city" covers six square miles, with more than three thousand constructions: temples, palaces, shrines, ceremonial platforms, large and small residences, ball courts, terraces, causeways, and plazas of varying sizes. The undersurface of the land is mainly limestone, which precludes digging wells for water. Drinking water in 1975 was collected from tin-roof rain runoff and stored in tanks. There was a museum, completed in 1964, a patio-style structure containing objects of pottery, bone, shell, and stone, mostly jade. Archaeologists sponsored by the University of Pennsylvania are credited for most discoveries.

The Jungle Inn is well equipped to handle overnight guests and I feel a three-day stay is necessary to do justice to this magnificent area. Our small group consisted of Americans from various states and an Indian guide. The guide was born near Tikal, and had worked excavating and restoring ruins for many years. He spoke excellent English. From him, we learned about the Mayan calendar, based on a fifty-two-year cycle that is accurate to within minutes in that period, as compared to our calendar, which needs a one-day adjustment every four years. At the inn, while waiting to depart, I had a few Gallo beers with a psychiatrist from California who offered me his services free when he heard I biked from New Jersey. Naturally, I refused as I felt he needed the service more than I did. As for the beer, I would rate Guatemalan suds just below Mexican *cerveza*. Of course, the time of day, heat, and my own temperature may influence my judgment. After walking the causeways and climbing to the top of Temples 1 and 2, I slept the entire return flight on the plane's rough bench seats, arranged along both sides of the craft.

Back in the capital, I strolled the streets to view the evening scene. Again, it is a land of contrasts: Mercedes Benzes pass by Indians in colorful dress, walking barefoot with their young in tow, one Indian family actually cooking over an open fire in the city plaza. Plenty of motorcycles, mostly Japanese, plus a sampling of Harleys and Triumphs. Local police rode mostly Harleys, unlike the Mexican cops, who straddled Hondas with worn-out tires. The business section looked like any business section, in any city, anywhere. Young lads cruising, and young lassies looking to be cruised. Lighted signs touting Carvel, Sears, Pepsi, Esso, Texaco, and any number of popular international products.

Early morning found me on the way out of Guatemala City and searching for the Pan American Highway. Most locals had never heard of this highway, but a young fellow going my way led me to Highway CA1, which is the Pan-Am. By mid morning I was ready to hassle my way out of Guatemala. Customs, *aduana*, police, etc., the complete battle lasted a good hour and a half. You stand in line waiting for the rubber stamp that will send you to the next rubber stamp. As I wandered through various rooms looking for somebody, anybody, to tend to my needs, I came across my agent, but he was busy necking with his girlfriend, so I discreetly retreated to my proper place at the end of the line. Naturally, I latched onto a young coyote to guide me through the maze. At each step of the ordeal I noticed attractive decals all over the place. The decals featured Quetzalcoatl, the feathered bird or serpent (take your choice) who was a traditional god or heroic figure of the ancient Aztecs. Actually, the quetzal is a bird of bright plumage, probably related to the parrot family. And at each step I asked if I might have one of said decals for Tinker's windshield, and always they said I could not have one. At the police stop, the fourth (I think they hate to see you leave), I asked my coyote if he could get one. He quickly ran back to the official of the first refusal and sure enough, he returned with four decals for me. Of course his tip brought forth the usual happy smile and sincere *gracias*. This particular coyote not only guided me through the hassles but he also guarded Tinker while I battled the rubber stamps. Some coyotes will exchange your money for the desired currency, but needless to say they will take a cut for the service. As I said before, all Central American countries will accept American dollars, sometimes, and for the most part countries will accept their neighbor's currency. But don't count on it. Don't accumulate excess amounts. While the Guatemalan border guards check all cars and buses, they also checked my bike, dirty laundry, and tools. Of course, each official collected a fee equal to forty cents to four dollars U.S.

From Guatemala I had planned a side trip to Belize (a Mayan word meaning "muddy water"), a very small country of about 8,700 square miles on the Caribbean coast. I changed my mind when informed the road was not passable. Tinker's weld job was still fresh in my mind and the road to Belize is rough in the best of times. Discretion being the better part of valor, I discretioned southward. On the road again for all of one hundred yards to the El Salvador aduana for my license and visa. With the help of another coyote, I was, to my surprise, escorted through without the usual hassle. The roads in El Salvador were not quite up to those of Guatemala. At one point I came upon a washed out bridge, and was forced to follow a bulldozed trail along the small river until a shallow area was found, and then, ride through the water and continue up the bank until connected to the main road. I felt this was worth a photo, so I sat and waited at least twenty minutes for a car to approach so I could get my shot. From the border, I found plenty of bumps and detours on gravel beds on the way to Santa Ana. Spotted a young fellow, so I stopped and asked him if the road was like this all the way to the city. He replied "sí, all good road." Couldn't find a hotel with security for the bike so I pressed on toward La Libertad, where I got my first glimpse of the Pacific Ocean and the lava-blackened sand of the beaches. The dirt roads along the beach are dotted with stands and huts, and I enjoyed a *langosta* dinner and a bottle of cool beer—all for $3.50 U.S. While supping, I was serenaded by two guitar-wielding singers. They were very good, so I overtipped by 50 cents. The cooking was done in a house across the street. The lonely hut-restaurant was occupied by one couple and myself.

La Libertad is a unique shallow-water port, with a long pier serviced by a narrow-gauge railroad. The soldier on guard duty at the warehouse gave me permission to park Tinker in a no-parking zone where he could keep an eye on it, as I strolled out on the pier. The dock hands skillfully lower cargo to lighters about forty feet below, which then transport the cargo to freighters that are anchored offshore in deeper water. As I surveyed the scene, a fishing boat approached, and was promptly hoisted by crane and tackle to the dock, and immediately, it was surrounded by locals who commenced to haggle over the price of the fish. Among the fish was a fair-sized shark, by now headless. After proffering the usual tip of a shiny colon ($.40 U.S.) and receiving the usual exuberant gracias, I retrieved Tinker and rode off into the sunset.

The fifty-mile side trip to La Libertad was well worth the effort. There is an old cliché that says, "Tourists travel to see the sights, and travelers travel to visit the people." Don't miss the opportunity to experience this rare bit of local flavor and be a traveler.

The Salvadorians were friendly, gracious, and generous. Don't let my meager tips fool you, I had been warned not to flaunt Yankee opulence. I've had youngsters, cops, and soldiers watch Tinker as I wandered the various neighborhoods. They did a great job and were ever grateful to earn a few extra centavos. Now on to San Salvador, the capital city of El Salvador, population then 500,000.

Of all the Central American "republics," El Salvador is the most densely populated. The people are mostly Ladino, that is, Europeanized Indians. A study of the climate, people, culture, economy, and history make for interesting reading. The Central American countries are often referred to as banana republics, and as of 1975 only the banana part was correct. The term originated because of wealthy U.S. corporations who owned the plantations and attempted to control the various governments. It became a term of disparagement.

I covered only 200 miles the next day because I couldn't get definite word on permits, visas, etc. to Honduras and Costa Rica, and so stayed put till the following day. Border personnel will process papers all day, but if you arrive at lunchtime siesta hours, be prepared to pay an extra fee.

Hit a nice hotel in the center of San Salvador with swimming pool, sauna, and air-conditioned rooms (a first on this trip). Took a swim in my $5.00 Guatemalan swim trunks and experienced a sauna for the first time in my life. I also had my first siege of Montezuma's revenge. Broke open my supply of Lomotil and, after the fourth dose, I felt on my way to normalcy. Had a fruit cup for dinner due to lack of desire for food. Fruit cup and a bottle of beer became a delightful dinner as I traveled Central America. All fresh fruit and enough to satisfy the most voracious appetite. Strolling around town, it seemed dead, or else I was at the wrong end of it. I returned to the hotel bar and caught up on my notes. Since I felt better, I had a few beers, hoping they wouldn't revive Montezuma. You get so thirsty and the folks are so friendly that you say, "Heck, I'll have another." About ten p.m., still at my barroom table engrossed in notes and beer, I suddenly realized the place had come alive. I guess my stroll was too early. Locals were now singing and dancing. If you travel the trails of Central America, plan some layovers and savor the local atmosphere. Temporarily the poverty, fear, bare-ass kids at play, and squalor seem miles away—but sadly they're not.

Still wallowing in my temporary luxury, I returned to my room and watched the first TV since Texas, the Flintstones in Spanish. Come to think of it, I haven't seen a headline in two weeks, and frankly, I haven't missed them. Since I only carry four changes of underclothes and socks, I must keep up with the laundry. Having done that before dinner, I draped them over the air conditioner and lamps to dry. Lesson Number 21: Don't dry clothes over lamps. My polyester socks burned from the heat of the bulb. Fortunately they did not flame, just kind of melted and stunk. The locals wouldn't appreciate your burning out a hotel for a pair of dirty socks. Now, one more dose of Lomotil and off to dreamland.

Early April 29, I departed my fancy quarters and headed back to reality. The bad news, more border hassles ahead; the good news, I'm running out of borders. Only three to go, and then home. While happily tooling down the highway (excuse me, trail), a motorcycle cop approached from the opposite direction and waved me to the side. Sensing an emergency, I moved as far to the right as the road would permit. Suddenly I was besieged by a million bicyclists—well, maybe a hundred or so. Seems the officer was escorting a bike marathon.

By this time, I was beginning to get a longing for home even though I enjoyed every mile of my trek, well almost every mile. Arrived at the Honduran border at mid morning. Getting out of one country and into the next could seem almost impossible. Imagine spraying Tinker's tires with aerosol cans of whatever at some crossings. Then, follow this act with stops at four departments (at least) for each exit and entry, where each one nails you for a fee of fifty cents to four dollars. Sometimes a receipt, sometimes no.

Took me one hour to clear the El Salvador border, but the entry to Honduras, not so long. While waiting for the Honduran agent to locate the proper rubber stamp, his pet baby parrot flew off. Since his flying ability was limited, we chased him down quickly. Possibly my help capturing his undersized pterodactyl eased my entry. From the border south, it's a nice, relatively level ride into Honduras, a land that Columbus claimed for Spain on his fourth journey to the new world. Stopped at a small home where they served thirst quenchers, and sat on the veranda chatting with an elderly Indian and his two grandchildren. Along came an aged Honduran on his donkey, and after taking his picture I attempted to have him pose on Tinker, while I would pose on his donkey. He would have none of this, and I learned later that he thought I wanted to swap my bike for his donkey. These short pit stops are always interesting, as most of the natives speak some semblance of English, and thus enhanced my knowledge of local lore.

Honduras I found not very exciting so I kept moving, and even bypassed a side trip to the capital city, Tegucigalpa. Rare is a capital city any place that doesn't have a railroad connection, so I guess Tegucigalpa qualifies as rare. Came upon a fork in the road and the sign had two names and two arrows, so arranged that you could apply either town to either arrow, and vice versa. As I attempted to solve this puzzle, a friendly local once again came to my rescue. He informed me that both arrows would lead me out of Honduras, but he recommended the one that would save me a couple of hours on the road. As I drift along the deserted roadway, excuse me, deserted trail, I remind myself to keep an eye peeled for a sight of two Mexican hikers. It seems they planned to fly to Argentina and then walk from Tierra del Fuego to Montreal, Canada, a total of 14,100 miles. They hoped to reach Montreal in time for the 1976 Olympic Games. I thought it was possible to meet them as their timing should put them somewhere along my route as I rode south. I never did discover whether their hike succeeded, or even happened.

To my surprise the Honduran border officials passed me through pronto, but my luck didn't last very long once the Nicaraguan aduana hierarchy latched onto me and Tinker. They gave me the biggest headache of the entire tour. Most border officials feel quite important and omnipotent, and that they are. They will determine when and if you can enter their domain. Of course you play the game by keeping your mouth shut while they process all the locals first. While I cooled my heels, trying my best to look like I love waiting, a bus pulled up and in comes the driver with about twenty passports, goes to the head of the line, and immediately the rubber stamps come to life. One impatient couple in a pickup from California was sent back to the previous consul due to improper papers. This could add a full day to your travels. Improper papers means your hair is too long, or some other silly excuse. Finally, the five- minute stamping job was promptly completed in one hour, with my pocket about four dollars lighter.

Drove on to León. No hotel, so I was forced to violate my own rule: Don't drive at night. After a very dark sixty miles, I arrived at Managua. While the gas tank was being refilled, once again a stranger came to my aid upon learning I was in search of a hotel, and led me to the one and only, the beautiful Hotel Continental. Throughout Nicaragua I experienced a definite anti-American feeling and yet I encountered more than a few episodes of complete strangers going out of their way to help me. This particular gentleman, when we arrived at the hotel, took the time to welcome me to Nicaragua, and wish me a nice stay. The ride in the dark was very tiring, which made my evening meal of fruit platter, coffee, and the inevitable beer, much tastier. The beer here is Carta Blanca or Victoria, both very good, but then the beer rating rises as the temperature does.

Next morning I taxied to the Costa Rican consulate. Why a taxi? Nobody could tell me where the office was, so I invested $3.00 in a cabby who knew the area. He found it, but it was closed, so later I attempted to return on the bike, which I had to kick-start as Tinker's battery had died, and then to add to the frustrations, I got lost. I did spy a Honda shop where I had the bone-dry battery refilled and recharged. Also had an oil change and a general checkup for Tinker. While waiting for the $3.50 service to be completed, the manager took me on a tour of his shop. He even thanked me for permitting him to practice his English. Another friendly Nicaraguan. The manager then had a young lad lead me to the Costa Rican consul where I completed the five-minute stamp job, which would at least allow me to get my foot in the door there. The devastation of Managua from the earthquake of 1972 was unbelievable. At the time of this visit, the city had been cleared of rubble and now looked like a giant football field. The marketplace now looked more like one of our larger flea markets. With all the help, financial and otherwise, from the US it's difficult to understand the lack of friendliness displayed by many officials.

A trip to the Panamanian consulate also seemed to be in order so as to ease my entry there. A visa is merely a stamp of approval, or an endorsement by officials saying in effect, "Proceed." It does not mean you can stay or that your vehicle doesn't need a license.

So why, after visiting the New York consul's office of each Central American country, do you have to hunt down their office at the border or in a neighboring country? The first visa gets your foot in the door, so you can now proceed to obtain your permit to stay three days or longer "with your vehicle." That's important, so don't try to leave without it. There is a very heavy tariff if you sell your vehicle, usually about 85%. Sound complicated? Even a joker with a Ph.D. in logic is helpless.

Now back on the road to Costa Rica and, about mid afternoon, I arrived at the border. Surprise of all surprises, every item was proper and I was permitted entry, free of charge. But alas, they did nail me $10.00 for Tinker's insurance. This was the one and only time my vehicle was insured in Central America. In Mexico, I tried to get insurance but was told I didn't need it. Vehicle insurance is often compulsory abroad, and it's wise to have it. I was overwhelmed by the courteous and friendly treatment. They do like bikes and were quite intrigued by Tinker's beeping directional signals, so I showed them every little feature of my 750cc Honda. Border officials are not usually very friendly to campers, trucks, or cars, which means everything is checked, but with the bike they checked absolutely nothing.

Columbus discovered Costa Rica ("rich coast") in 1502. He gave it this name because he anticipated riches such as gold and jewels. He found little, if any. Costa Rica is one of the smaller C.A. countries, about 200 miles top to bottom, and roughly 125 miles wide. Central Costa Rica, called the Meseta Central, is a plateau up to 5,000 feet high, offering a very moderate climate, while the low-lying coastal plains are hot all year. The mountain regions are cool, sometimes downright cold. Rainfall approaches

120 inches per year. No precious metals meant few Spanish colonists. At the time of independence in 1821, the population was less than 75,000. It was the first C.A. country to build railroads and paved highways. These connected the capital, San José, to Panama. Costa Rica was, or is, or may be, the closest thing to a democracy in all of Central America. From my pre-trip readings, I looked forward to seeing the traditional oxcarts, with their colorfully painted carts, but alas, all I saw was rubber-tired oxcarts. The only traditional cart I spied was, I suspect, for the benefit of us tourists.

And now on to Puntarenas, on the Pacific coast, where I found a motel with guard on duty all night, so Tinker was safe on the assigned sidewalk spot. Strolled the pier area and viewed the freighters anchored off-shore. The caretaker assured me the area was safe, and I'm sure it was as all the people I met seemed to confirm this. I ran into a woman and son from Nebraska who were checking out retirement possibilities. Costa Rica seems to be a favorite retirement area for many Americans. Favorable weather, low cost of living, and similar population mix to ours encourages this shift of population.

Took a swim in the three-foot-deep, leaf-cluttered pool and then adjourned to a *pollo frito* and beer dinner. I'll just have to learn more Spanish, as I'm getting tired of fried chicken. This small motel (spelled "hotel") charged $9.00 U.S. per night, breakfast included.

A tropical downpour woke me during the night, the first rain since Tennessee. At sunrise I took in Puntarenas from my bike, watched an old transplanted Staten Island ferry plying its way across the harbor (saving travelers an 80-mile drive), and then caught sight of the narrow-gauge electric train arriving from San José. Now I headed for San José. My plans called for a layover in the capital, while I took a bus tour to the Irazú volcano, but I couldn't find a hotel with adequate vehicle protection so I headed for Cartago. A young policeman pulled me over and in fractured

English informed me that he must issue me a ticket. I kept giving him "no comprendo." I knew he meant I wasn't wearing my helmet, so after a few more "no comprendos," I put my lid on, and in utter frustration he told me to vamoose, or something, so I did, in the direction of Cartago. A lack of tourists meant no tour bus to the volcano, so I decided to go by bike.

Now the Irazú volcano is ten-, eleven- or twelve-thousand five-hundred feet up, take the number you like. The sign at the summit says 12,500 feet, but in Central America don't pay too much attention to signs. At any rate it's almost twenty-five miles of winding, twisting roads, where even the potholes have potholes, before you reach the cloud-shrouded peak of the double-coned volcano (though I could only see one cone). I was the only human at the top. It was an eerie, cold experience. Took a few photos and said good-bye to Irazú. Halfway down I stopped at an alpine-like cabin for a quiet lunch. Finally, at sea level, while removing my heavier jacket, a police car stopped and the officers asked how I was. I told them I was looking for Highway C2, and they graciously escorted me through town and onto the highway. Thank God they were there to help, as I might still be drifting around the unexciting town of Cartago.

Sixty miles south of Cartago lies the city of San Isidro de General. Once again I found myself up in the mountains surrounded by clouds so thick I needed the headlights. Freezing cold, eerie, spooky, scary, an experience hopefully not to be repeated. As Tinker's gas supply reached the reserve level, San Isidro appeared and I came across a nice hotel. The manager permitted me to park Tinker in the alley to his private quarters, and after a refreshing shower I walked the empty town square. Had dinner at the hotel: chop suey, beer, and more beer.

San Isidro apparently is a convenient stopover for those traveling to and from Panama, and thus warrants such a nice spacious hotel. While relaxing and doing notes I suddenly realized the place was beginning to fill up and getting a little noisy. Costa Rican people seem to be much like those of the US. They are generally more fair than in other countries of Central America, but there is a good number of blacks too, mostly from the Caribbean islands. There are few of Indian ancestry. Many U.S. citizens find comfortable retirement in Costa Rica; the weather is very favorable, as is the cost of living, and the English language is almost universal.

So far, at the right time I seem to meet the right people to guide me in the proper direction, police, civilians, or military. The only exceptions—most (but not all) border officials. The worst, without a doubt, were the would-be dictators in Nicaragua. As the locals continue to party, I'm off to the arms of Morpheus (he the god of dreams, son of Hypnos, the god of sleep). Only covered 200 miles today, due to the creepy side trip to Irazú.

With an early start I hoped to reach the border before siesta time and thus avoid being nailed a few extra colons, cordovas, pesos, or whatever. After a sound, long sleep and a short breakfast, I was on the road again, and a pretty good road it is, with few or no mountains. The petrol here is a higher grade and also more expensive. I approached the Panamanian border at mid morning. Cleared the Costa Rica side with no sweat. In fact the officials kept an eye on Tinker while I changed all my leftover pesos, quetzals, colons, lempiras, etc. for U.S. dollars at a convenient border bank. The Panama balboa is equal to one American dollar, and they use our bills but their own silver coins. And now, since Panama considers herself part of South America we are about to leave Central America.

Officials at the Panamanian border seem to be the most efficient, with the least amount of red tape, although there are four checkpoints between the Costa Rican border and Panama City. Don't fail to stop, as they must check your papers and enter your name, etc. in their souvenir book.

I overshot my next stop, Santiago, then overshot Aguadulce, accidentally spotting a motel, and there I was only a short distance from Panama City. My route in Panama was fairly level on comparatively good roads. Panama's mountains are mostly toward the Caribbean side, leaving the rest of the country suitable for the large coffee and banana plantations. I would have continued to the capital but the clock jumps ahead one hour at this point, and that would have meant a rush hour arrival. Not knowing what traffic to expect and remembering the chaos in Mexico City, I decided to stay the night and relax, and get an early start. Plenty of time for a nice shower, then a martini while I caught up on my notes. In the previous few days, I had experienced severe gusts of wind, creating unbelievable dust. In the misty mountains I had frozen, only to boil in the sea-level heat.

After Costa Rica you have fewer and fewer oxcarts, donkeys, and human toters, and more and more tractors, diesel-chugging trucks and light motorcycles, but still plenty of bareback cowboys. At one point I thought I was suffering delusions, as the sun seemed to be in the wrong position. If you are traveling south in early afternoon the sun should be slightly to your right or approximately two o'clock, but now it was at nine o'clock. I stopped and checked the map, and sure enough, the isthmus at this point curves northeast. Surprisingly, the Caribbean entrance to the Panama Canal is farther west than the Pacific end.

The final 100 miles seemed slow in coming but, alas, as I rounded a bend in the road, there, off in the distance, sat the "Bridge to South America." I felt ecstatic. Here I was about to achieve my goal. I could almost "see the elephant." So I crossed the bridge and immediately made a wrong turn and wound up near Clayton Air Force Base. Surveyed the base and then wandered over to the Miraflores Locks, which control entry to the canal from the Pacific side. Timing was perfect—a German ship was just approaching. So I sat in the tower and listened to a piped-in commentary of the entire procedure. Ships enter under their own power, but are guided through the lock by locomotives called "mules." A trip to Panama is not complete without a visit to the locks. To get a mental picture of the canal, nicknamed the "Big Ditch," picture the Pacific and the Caribbean at mean sea level. The canal and Gatún Lake are about 85 feet above sea level. From the Pacific, ships enter the Miraflores locks (two sets), which raise the ship to the 54-foot level. Next, the Pedro Miguel lock (one set), raises the ship another 31 feet, and the ship then sails the canal and Gatún Lake. When ready to leave the canal, the ship enters the Gatún Locks (three sets), which lower it 85 feet to sea level and it sails off into the sunrise. It takes eight to ten hours to traverse the canal, at an average cost of $30,000 in 1975. Very large ships will pay many times that amount and it is well worth the cost. Consider that the canal saves the 8,000-mile journey down and around the stormy tip of South America, not to mention the additional days at sea.

I drifted into the center of town and registered at the Hotel International, a grand hotel in its day, a fleabag in mine. Later I discovered that most or all the modern hotels were on the outskirts of the city. Food was expensive and not exactly gourmet. It so happened that I arrived on Panama's Labor Day so I must wait one more day before sending Tinker home via freighter and I must now extend my vehicle permit for another day or two. That translates into more paperwork, and more visits to the local dictators.

With time on my hands, I paid a rainy visit to Antigua Panamá (more ruins). One church in Antigua supposedly has a gold-plated altar which was painted to disguise it, in anticipation of a visit by the feared pirate Henry Morgan. The desk clerk, going off duty, led me to the telegraph office for a phone call home. The wonderful treatment at this modest place caused me to change my mind regarding a move to a more modern hotel. This clerk refused to leave me until he was assured that I needed no more assistance. Then a short visit to the casino, where I needed no assistance in a losing spin of the roulette wheel.

Since they were using the enclosed parking area for holiday ceremonies, the hotel guard put Tinker on the sidewalk in front of the hotel. Very convenient, although it did look a little out of place. Dinner at 7:00 p.m. in a fancy dining room occupied by three diners—myself and two waiters. Prices were high, so little wonder diners were few.

My May 2 schedule called for a visit to the consulate to have the vehicle permit extended and then a trip to Colón to hopefully put Tinker on board for the sail home. During the fifty-two mile route, Panama City to Colón, I had to sit out a tropical squall. Then I spied what looked like a body lying on the side of the road, but it turned out to be a sloth, this followed by a car stalled in a flooded section of the road. A truck driver and myself, knee-deep in water, pushed him to dry land so we could both pass. Adding to the frustration, the shipping company informed me that I would have to return to Balboa to ship the bike. The road between Colón and Balboa parallels the canal but you get only a glimpse of Gatún Lake here and there. To better view the entire canal, ride the train. The official who directed me to Colón must have taken lessons from the Mexicans, but I did get to see a part of Panama that I wouldn't have otherwise.

Back in the Canal Zone I innocently entered the army base, and was duly saluted by the guard. During three years service in the army, this old corporal was never saluted by anybody, so I felt pretty important as I had the gas tank filled with G.I. petrol at one half the off-base cost. Some mistakes are too much fun to make only once.

Finally, I found the shipping company and quickly learned that less cubic feet equals less shipping cost, so I proceeded to remove fairing, saddlebags, lower handle bars, etc. The estimate to sail Tinker to Miami and then truck it to New York was $300 dollars, so I opted for the slow boat to Brooklyn for $200. The native who did the crating was tickled to accept my offer of the five-gallon tank of gas. Once again a toothy "gracias." During paper processing, the manager, upon learning I was from Jersey, introduced me to a fellow Jerseyite, a Rev. Frederico McTiernan. The Rev was an army chaplain, and during assignment to Panama, had recognized the dire need for mission help in this area. He later resigned his army commission and requested assignment to the Panama missions. The Rev originally hailed from Elizabeth, N.J., and we had more than a few mutual Hibernian friends from the Bayonne area. He was also related to two of my patients. A small world. Without Tinker, I was now totally alone and looking for anyone to befriend me and keep me headed in the right direction. Look no further. Fr. McTiernan took me under his wing as we developed a lasting friendship. Since then we have traded visits to my home and to his retirement abode in Bricktown, both in New Jersey. Father chauffeured me to the mission for dinner, and after meeting all eight priests of the parishes and mission, delivered me to my pad to complete my notes and sip a relaxing brew.

While driving, Padre filled me in on the native situation and history. He says, and I quote, "We converted the Panama Catholics to Christianity." Very few (20% in 1975) were married; they just live together and raise a family, but probably would marry but for the lack of priests. These are religious people and vocations would be no problem except for celibacy. Father instituted a CYO, Pre-Cana program, and Cursillo. When asked how long a person could go without sex, some of the people answered from two days to two weeks. An elderly woman said two weeks. Reminded me of the lady I met on a bus in Guatemala City who climbed aboard with three sets of twins. I asked her if she always had twins. She replied, "Oh no, lots of times we don't get nothing." One major problem, in my opinion, is the obsession too many of the young macho teens have with the need to prove their manhood by making a gal pregnant. There are some who feel the need to prove it each year.

On one tour I accompanied Fr. Mac and two other priests on a visit to their MD. I had a nice chat with him. The doctors have an impressive professional building with pharmacy and attached clinic. Panama has a good health program. All workers are covered by a form of social security and medicare. The physicians have private clinics, but state clinics are available with excellent care for outlanders. Everybody works and everybody eats. Aside, Padre pointed out a sanctioned cathouse (sanctioned by whom?), as we traversed the area. The missions mentioned earlier were started from scratch by a handful of priests from the diocese of Chicago and by then involved six parishes.

The area of Fr. McTiernan's parish, a short drive from Panama City, is settled by squatters who all work but pay no rent. Water is delivered by tank truck daily. A few wells are available and residents must wait in line one or more hours for a pail of water. The squalor of Panama City was equaled only by that of Colón. Yet there was also plenty of commercial and condominium construction. Although they appeared to be at the saturation point then, it continues today. The cost of living is quite high in Panama City and the surrounding area, complicated by the difference in wage scales between the Canal Zone, which paid U.S. minimum scale, and the Panamanian scale of roughly fifty cents per hour. Kind of adds to the "have" and "have not" situation.

It's May 3 and I'm quickly running out of time. I had originally planned to travel home via freighter, or tramp steamer, but the earliest ship heading for the New York area, Albany to be exact, wouldn't be ready for departure until another week. Freighters accept up to twelve passengers, due to maritime regulations. Usually there is an age restriction, probably because of health concerns. They are said to provide good food, and fares are very reasonable. The schedules are also very iffy, as the ship may be called to dock at any port en route to pick up additional cargo. It was disappointing to have to pass up this opportunity. So now, if and when Panama will release me, I'll schedule a flight home. As with all Central American countries, if you enter with a vehicle you must leave with the same vehicle. As I mentioned earlier, if you sell it you must pay a heavy tariff, up to 85%. And so I must wait for Tinker to be aboard ship before I can leave Panama.

While being held hostage I decided to visit the San Blas Islands (officially Archipiélago de las Mulatas). A very small twelve-passenger plane, half-filled (or half-empty, the choice is yours), landed me there in about one hour. These islands, numbering about four hundred, lie off the Caribbean coast of Panama and are occupied by the Cuna Indians. These interesting, usually short, dark-complexioned people possess the highest albino rate in the world, about two percent. The women wear gold rings in their noses (one ring per nose) and cover their chests with reverse appliqués called *molas*. These in turn, very often, are decorated with hammered gold squares. Supposedly, the piles of coconuts stacked in the corners of their thatch-roof huts are an indication of personal wealth, never mind the nasal gold rings and their gold plates. The aforementioned molas are exquisite examples of the artistic ability of the Cuna women. These appliqués are approximately twelve by fifteen inches, featuring colorful designs of fishes and birds, among others. Before leaving the islands I bargained with the natives and wound up with five. The young male Cunas are big on basketball, despite their small stature, and they must play on dirt courts. Most of the islands are very small and uninhabited, but they keep one sizeable island where they grow limited crops and another where they bury the dead. Of course, their personal islands, you are not permitted to visit. The main island sports the Hotel Banai, more cabin than hotel, which offers overnight facilities. I could see no reason to overnight.

My tour group included a honeymooning couple from Belgium, two stragglers, myself, and our guide, who happened to be one of the two percent, a true albino Cuna Indian. He led us on a visit to three neighboring islands via large dugout canoe with a very modern Mercury outboard engine and then back to the Hotel Banai for a lobster dinner. If you are inclined, you may dive into the inlet and capture your own lobster, but I did not feel so inclined. The Cuna children and adults all willingly pose for photos for a small payment. Kids wait on dock for the returning tourists so they can dive and retrieve tossed coins. The water is very clear, so no problem. The San Blas Islands are not exactly a tourist mecca, but they are definitely worth a visit.

After the lobster meal, I snoozed in a nearby hammock as I awaited the plane for my return to Panama City. Relaxing in the hammock reminded me of the time while riding in El Salvador as nightfall set in when I encountered a couple of fair-size animals enjoying the warmth of the macadam. With my own safety in mind, I chose a nice spot to string my $4.00 hammock betwixt two trees and slept the night away, with no ticks, land crabs, or people, only the stars.

The less-than-one-hour return flight was via a five-passenger Apache, with two elderly ladies from Brooklyn. The pistol-packing pilot invited me to occupy the copilot seat, and what a beautiful sight it was as we flew through bumpy thunderheads. This small local airline had a none too good record, three crashes in one year. This I learned after my return. Some of the Cuna work on the mainland and return each weekend. They often carry a few passengers as standees, overloading the small planes. Like the buses in Panama, overcrowded and usually poorly maintained.

Back in the city I took a walking tour of the downtown area, seeing many familiar trade names, such as Sears. I checked out a few, smoke-filled taverns but didn't enter as I felt no need to press my luck at this stage. Now back to my suite as I felt the need for another dose of Lomotil, to ease my second attack of the "Toltec two-step." Not as bad as the first one.

Sunday, I taxied out to San Miguelito parish for 9:00 a.m. Mass which started promptly at 9:35 a.m. Fr. Fred explained he must wait till all are here. Singing, accompanied by guitar, was simply beautiful. During the homily, Padre called me to the altar and introduced me to his congregation as "mi amigo un poco loco" and explained how I had come down from the US by *moto*. With permission, I took photos during Mass and also a few of the elderly woman who had made the exquisite altar linens which were being used for the first time. Following the Pater Noster, the sign of peace was something to behold. A bear hug from each and every one present left me weakened but joyful. A truly spiritual feeling. These people gave a total stranger everything they had, love.

Following Mass, I accompanied Father as we canvassed the shantytown in search of workers to help complete the erection of the Catholic Center—a one-room affair with a dirt floor. We worked, with many volunteers, until mid-afternoon and even with private instruction in the handling of the machete, I fear I was of little help. We all enjoyed the lunch of watery soup prepared by one of the dedicated women. Any food served with the dedication and love of these women is magna-gourmet. Met Bishop Marcos McGrath when he visited to offer his moral support. Since I was so inept with the machete, I was assigned to check out a 100cc Honda for one of the priests. After a quick tune-up the bike purred like a kitten, and I was immediately elevated to sainthood. Well, they did say thanks.

The priests of all six parishes meet for dinner with the Bishop each Sunday and I was invited. The power of Fr. McTiernan. Once again I had the opportunity to converse with the bishop. I found him extremely personable, if quite nationalistic. I understand he was born in Panama of American parents. He heads a diocese, operating well as a diocese should.

After dinner I was chauffeured through the shantytown and dropped in on a number of hospitable people as Father visited his flock. At one stop, a couple were celebrating their sixth anniversary and Father had been invited to stop by. I was previously advised to accept all offerings, no matter how meager, and so I graciously accepted two highballs in paper cups and pieces of chicken on paper plates. At times like this, my only wish is for millions of dollars so I could repay all these people of God. If I wasn't happily married with four children, I would seriously consider a vocation to the missions of Panama, despite the politically motivated signs reading Yankee Go Home.

Returning after a full day, we visited an old army buddy of Father, a lieutenant colonel in the Canal Zone. Had a couple of Tom Collinses (remember I have a chauffeur and thus am not driving) served in fancy crystal ware and, you know, my paper cup highballs were just as tasty, maybe more. The colonel was memorable, to me, mainly because after returning to the States I was able to mail needed motorcycle parts to all the cycling priests via the colonel. In other words, US to the American Canal Zone equaled no border, no international hassles. The colonel would then deliver the goods to the local priests.

Before leaving the San Miguelito area I must dwell a few moments on the parish of Cristo Redento. The Archdiocese of Chicago founded and staffed the Panama Mission. As stated earlier the mission had grown to six parishes, each with its own church, but not structures as we see in the States. Since they lack air-conditioning, the buildings usually sport a raised roof and open-structured walls to permit plenty of airflow

The church of Cristo Redento in San Miguelito contains six murals of various sizes and magnificent artistry and the thoughtful meanings expressed in these murals is a story I could not do justice to, but I will try to describe one: "The Waters of Life" on the wall of the baptistry. The burning bush is reflected in the figure of Moses, who, moved by the power of the Spirit, sees past, present, and future. His left hand changes from leprous to healthy. His right hand grasps a snake which changes to a staff, releasing the waters of life. Sickness, death, and evil, are overcome by the creation of new life. From a womb-like cloud comes forth a multitude, welcoming the newly baptized into the embrace of the community. All the murals in the church of Cristo Redento were created by artist Lillian Brulc, a native of Joliet, Illinois. She has received master of fine arts degrees from both the School of the Art Institute of Chicago and the University of Chicago. The artistic beauty and their stimulating and thoughtful interpretation made the trip to Panama even more memorable.

Two Panamanian sculptors collaborated in the completion of the altar and baptismal font. "Che" Torres, a resident of the San Miguelito area, sculpted the baptismal font of native stone, employing forms meaningful in the daily life of the people. Rubén Arboleda, a resident of Chilibre, sculpted the altar from a single log of *cedro espino*, a native Panamanian wood.

Back in Panama City, I treated for dinner, no big deal — a $14.00 tab for four, including drinks. My friends delivered me to my scratchpad at nine o'clock p.m. and there we said our good-byes. But not before I made arrangements to have a Mass of Thanksgiving said in answer to my family's prayers and my sister's Novena for a safe journey. They were well answered.

Next morning it took me two hours to locate a bank that would honor my letter of credit. This is a useful item that you obtain from your local bank, assuming of course that you have an account at said bank. Basically they freeze the amount you specify, which is secured for your use only. One problem was that most of the Central American banks at this time claimed they never heard of them.

Due to the rapidly evaporating time factor, I hired a cabby to stay with me through my final hassles. Taxi drivers rent a taxi on a per-day basis and then hope to gather enough fares to meet the day's expenses, roughly 16 balboas (that is, 16 dollars). After paying my shipping bill, the bill of lading was ready by early afternoon. At the consular office to pick up my exit permit, I was informed that the bill of lading must be the original copy. So now back to the shipping clerk. Got the U.S. immigration officer to help. No problem says he, and he gets his Panamanian counterpart to stamp "original" on the very same paper. Suddenly

I'm legal. Tomorrow I'll hit the consular office early and hopefully get to the airport on time.

My helpful cabby did just that with two hours to spare. Our agreed price for two days of back-and-forth travel from one end of the city to the other amounted to twenty-five balboas. I never could have found the various offices I needed for clearance without his help. Once again, he stuck to the agreed fee but this time I insisted on raising the ante. While waiting for Braniff to arrive from Colombia, I hit the slots for five dollars. Now I was ready to depart.

The flight over Cuba and on to Miami was as smooth as the martini I sipped as I ate dinner. Sometimes I wish I hadn't taken this trip. Why? Because the scenes of poverty, squalid living conditions, destruction by earthquakes, mud slides, and flooding, plus political unrest, left me with a feeling of helplessness, frustration, and empathy. With my antipathy toward organized charities with ultrahigh operating expenses that leave minimal amounts for the needy, I extend my meager charitable budget to agencies such as the Salesian Missions, etc., feeling assured that each peso is directed to the mission's aim.

The short layover in Miami offered enough time to clear customs, with my camera bag and Fr. McTiernan's suitcase filled with trinkets and beads, heading to his young relatives. I had no luggage otherwise, as I had washed and given away my badly worn socks and some other things. Also had just enough time to call home with the arrival time, etc., and snatch a quick glass of American beer.

The Miami-to-Newark flight served dinner, so now I have eaten two dinners in four hours, and of course a like number of martinis. I had an interesting view of a thunderstorm from above as we passed over Virginia. It is 8:00 p.m., and the sky is beginning to close in as my Panama adventure draws to a close. And as my jaunt nears its end I would like to personally thank the tour guides, police officers, soldiers, taxi drivers, Fr. McTiernan and his fellow priests, the general populace, and most importantly the "coyotes," those little guys who were so helpful getting me out of one country and into the next. Their grateful smiles and gracias for the precious little "teeps" they received were enough to make my heart tingle. After deplaning in Newark, my wife Elsie, son Joe, and sister Eleanor were there to meet me. It sure was great to see them. This beautiful experience will be hard to duplicate, but still, a greater feeling is to be back home in one piece. Because all my family's prayers were answered, I did get to see the "elephant," or in this case, "el elefante."

Five weeks after my return, Tinker sailed into New York Harbor and docked at a Brooklyn pier. It seems ironic that Tinker got to sail home via freighter, while I had to fly. In a borrowed van I drove to the pier to pick up Tinker—a simple task. Well, not exactly, since there was one last hassle lurking for me. Having experienced the modus operandi in the Jersey dock area while delivering Coca Cola for shipment aboard liners and cruise ships, I wasn't surprised to find that I must tip each and every hand stuck out in front of me. (While attending St. Louis U, I spent my summers working for the Coca Cola Company.) I was assigned a worker to locate my crate and facilitate its clearance through immigration. Similar to the coyotes in Central America, except these jokers don't deal in quarters. They are well paid but literally hold you up for $10.00, or more. I gave up ten dollars and it did get me through pretty quick. Even the forklift operator brazenly asked, "What about me?" as he held my crated Tinker on high. With Tinker's safety in mind, I surrendered a $5.00 ransom. American dockworkers make the Central American bandidos look like pikers. After a cursory inspection by Immigration (no tip necessary), I was happy to depart bandit land and return to New Jersey.

With Tinker safely tucked away in his own pad I had time to recall a few statistics. The entire trip to Panama covered twenty-eight days. It included more than 6,000 miles on Tinker and

3,300 miles via plane (the side trips to Tikal and the San Blas Islands, plus the flight home). The miles were spread over seven of our states and seven Latin American countries. More important than the statistics, the memories of the scores of kind, helpful, and openhearted people I met throughout the journey will be with me forever.

IV.
Reflections

As a teen, one of my favorite pastimes was daydreaming. And my favorite time for daydreaming was during sophomore high school English literature class. In my dreams I would envision lots of things, but mostly exciting travels through the West and other exotic places. Unfortunately, these tours were usually interrupted by the sudden crack of Sister's yardstick across the desk. In our youth we dream of the future and as we grow older we dream of the past, but now we call it reminiscing. During one of these periods of reminiscing, a special ride came to mind.

It occurred during the summer in the year 1979. At that time I was the KofC Grand Knight of Council 6903, Prospect Park, N.J., and the Knights of Columbus National Convention was scheduled for San Diego, Calif. Also, at that time I had enrolled in a concentrated course in acupuncture, as related to dentistry.

The seminar, sponsored by the University of Southern California, just happened to be offered in Los Angeles. The next step was to make plans for my wife to fly out, since she had an adverse attitude toward two-wheelers, and meet me at our retreat, the Beverly Hilton.

With my wife's reservations taken care of, I mounted Tinker Four and headed west. Once out of the metropolitan New York and North Jersey area the roads were mine, almost. With the usual short stops to visit friends, the miles passed by quickly. Very often I followed the so-called business routes which steer you through the center of various-sized towns. Usually these smaller towns offered better buys for motels and restaurants, and more intimate glimpses of the locals. At one layover along old Route 40, somewhere in Indiana, I checked into a motel and after registering I inquired as to where I could find a local diner or restaurant for dinner. Since it was late, my host informed me that all eateries were probably closed but she would check. After a brief phone call to a local beanery, she told me they were ready to close but would wait if I came right down. And quickly, down I went. In spite of the inconvenience I caused, I was treated like a VIP at this quite fashionable restaurant. Where else but in a small town?

With a multitude of possible interruptions, such as thunderstorms, construction areas, accidents, etc., I usually allowed ample time to reach my destination. Sometimes an interesting tourist trap would warrant a brief interruption from the monotony of the interstates.

As I approached St. Louis, the imposing sight of the Gateway Arch triggered an acute case of nostalgia, so I decided to spend the night there. I knew the itinerary, including hotel stops, of a tour group from my hometown, and since they would be in St. Louis at this time, I booked into the same hotel. It was very early, so I took me and Tinker down to the arch and rode to the top (*sans* Tinker) for a beautiful view of the Mississippi and surrounding countryside from the 600-foot-high observation platform. During my student days at St. Louis U the arch was just a dream, but the two old-timers, the courthouse and the small church, were well-known landmarks. They are presently located next to the arch. More accurately the arch was constructed above the old landmarks. The church was built in 1832 and the courthouse is noted for the rendering of the Dred Scott Decision (time to check your high school American history notes.) When I returned to the hotel the tour group had already arrived, so I enjoyed a pleasant dinner and social with my North Haledon, N.J., friends before retiring.

Early next morning as the tour bus headed east, on its final leg of a twenty-eight-day U.S. tour, I headed west toward my next stop, a small town at the far end of Oklahoma. It was a pleasant jaunt of 500 miles interrupted by a brief, but active, dust storm that forced a short off-road rest.

After departing Sooner country, I drifted off course in a northerly direction, a drifting habit I acquired many years ago. I following Rte. 472 until I connected to I-25 and by day's end I found myself in Pueblo, Colorado, where I grabbed a good night's sleep.

A short ride from Pueblo will take you to Manitou, at the base of Pikes Peak. The climb to the 14,000-foot peak is not a bad drive, but the downward trek can be tough on the brakes, so with Tinker's well-being in mind, I opted for the cog railway. Tinker had many more miles to travel before this trip was complete. Once atop the peak you are rewarded with a pass through an ice path (early summer) to a cafeteria and gift shop. Here I witnessed a guest with gasping breath, another with a bleeding nose, and many asking, When do we go down? Don't let me discourage you, it is a very worthwhile trip and I highly recommend it to all. The visit to the peak used up most of the day, so after a short jaunt I checked into a small motel for the night.

After breakfast, I followed I-25 south to Route 160 which offers a wonderful, scenic ride, especially for motorcycles, as you head west across southern Colorado. At various points along this trail, shelters are built over the road to ward off snow tumbling down the mountainsides. I continued on 160 to Durango. I love train rides, so I attempted to make a reservation for the

Durango-Silverton narrow-gauge train tour. Unfortunately, it was booked out for the day. So I hopped on Tinker and headed for Mesa Verde National Park. An almost circular path around Mesa Verde provides excellent views of the cliff dwellings, built by ancestors of the Pueblo Indians. Some of these were built as early as A.D. 450. The cliffs provided shelter from enemies and harsh weather conditions. Mesa Verde offers very interesting and unusual attractions, so if you are in the area, go for it. A visitor should plan spending at least one full day enjoying this relic of the past. It should whet your appetite for further knowledge, as it did mine.

I can't recall, returning from any ride, that I didn't head for the big book to enhance my knowledge of the attractions I had visited. After each experience, I promise to study up *before* I visit these sites, but alas, since I rarely plan my itinerary that well, it always ends up the same way: arrive home, greet family, grab the big book and read, and relive my experience.

A not-too-long drive in a southwesterly direction brings you to "Four Corners." It's the only point in the US where four states meet at one point (Colorado, Utah, Arizona, and New Mexico). A big nothing, so don't waste your time. Keep moving and save your spare time for Bryce Canyon, Zion National Park, and Monument Valley, which are located a short distance from the "Corners." Of course, keep in mind that "a short distance" in our western states can mean a few hundred miles.

Bryce Canyon happens to be one of my favorite pictures of God's handiwork. You will be amazed at the variety of red and pink shades of the sculptured rock domes and spires. The canyon walls are filled with endless formations. Although I had visited the canyon on a previous ride, I just couldn't resist a return trip.

But now I must press forward as I have already used up most of the spare time I had allotted. From Bryce Canyon I sought out I-15 and headed for Los Angeles. Since L.A. was still more than 500 distant miles, I checked into a motel in the first town

I hit on I-15, which was just beyond the Arizona border. An early start would put me in the Los Angeles area about noon, so I resisted the temptations of Vegas and continued on across the Mojave Desert. I just love deserts—the tantalizing allure of these wonderful wastelands, I cannot resist. As a result I find myself parking Tinker a safe distance off the road and wandering about, in my solitude, taking care not to tread on an ole sidewinder's[6] territory.

Well everything went smoothly after my early start until I reached the Los Angeles freeways. Los Angeles Pandemonium would say it better. Scary moments followed more scary moments, and suddenly I arrived at the Beverly Hilton. We all know Los Angeles is a very large city, land- wise, and after a little research I was amazed to find that this city covers 468 square miles. I figured this must be the largest city in the country, but alas, wrong again, it seems Jacksonville, Fla., with 827 square miles, has one of the largest areas of any city in the United States. Another source credits Jacksonville with a mere 759 square miles.

As I rolled into the entrance of this fancy hotel, I spied a group of pylons, probably a reserved area for VIP arrivals. So I rode betwixt the cones and climbed off Tinker to face whatever you call a parking lot maitre d', dressed like a decorated general, who rumbled toward me while bellowing, "You can't park there." When he got close, I asked, "Do you treat all your guests this way?" Suddenly he calmed down and politely asked if I had a reservation. I replied, equally politely, "Yes, I do, and I'll be needing someone to carry my bags, and guide me to a safe area to park." Now he was befuddled and wasn't sure to whom he was talking, but he did order one of his underlings to guide me to a safe place to park Tinker. Since one of my saddlebags had cracked during some bumpy riding during the past weeks, I insured against further damage by tying it with clothesline that I had

6   A sidewinder is a small rattlesnake. It gets its name from the way it slithers sideways across the desert floor.

purchased en route. It was embarrassing to have a porter drop my bags at the front desk, with one of them tied up that way. Now I'll have you know, my saddlebags were the latest model and design for the Honda Gold Wing, and while they looked pretty they just didn't withstand the vibrations of long road trips. Anyway, with Tinker safely tucked in, and me and my bags transported to my posh quarters, I was all set to grab a little shut-eye.

Lo and behold, there was my wife, Elsie, busily unpacking: She had arrived a half hour earlier. First order of the day, a trip to the local liquor depot for a bottle of the bubbly stuff, next a quiet celebration in our exquisite abode.

Bright and early next morning, I experienced my first session of the thirty-hour acupuncture course. The class consisted of eighteen students, so we were assured of ample individual assistance as needed. Completion of the course and the presentation of a very pedantic-looking certificate was just enough excuse for a return visit to the booze emporium for more champagne and, of course, a more earnest celebration.

As usual the dawn arrived too early, but schedules must be kept, so as my wife headed for San Diego by air, I mounted Tinker and searched through the freeway maze for I-5, which would lead me to San Diego and the national convention of the Knights of Columbus. By the time I covered the 125 miles to San Diego, my wife had already booked in, unpacked, and was ready to do the convention thing: celebrate with fancy cocktail parties, overeat rich foods, and then fling ourselves into the arms of Morpheus, dream god. Despite the three days of meetings, banquets, etc., we did manage a side trip to Tijuana, Mexico, an interesting but all too short visit.

With a most enjoyable convention behind us, I left my wife in the company of a fellow Knight and his wife, who also happened to be neighbors of ours in New Jersey, for the return flight. While I headed east on I-8, my Frau enjoyed a visit to the Johnny Carson Show and a Los Angeles Rams preseason session. It seems our neighbor had a son with good connections. And so, after a lonely 200 miles I arrived in Yuma, Arizona. Remembering the many cowboy films I enjoyed in my youth (the name Yuma seemed synonymous with the "oaters"), I just had to visit this old town. When I exited the highway, I was greeted by a major construction area, and then what I saw did not resemble what I had in mind so I pulled into a fast-food outlet for a refreshing Coke. It was a very hot day and I later discovered that Yuma set the national high for that particular day, 114 degrees F. So much for Yuma. A short distance west of Tucson, I-8 joins I-10. Disillusioned, I rode off on I-10 toward the New Mexico border and after about 400 boiling hot miles I anxiously searched for a motel in Lordsburg, New Mexico. While searching, those familiar flashing lights appeared behind me. A very friendly Indian trooper informed me that I had no taillight. He even stopped traffic as I crossed the street to a motel, another example of the kind, helpful people I've encountered in my travels. I booked into the motel and was politely informed that the restaurant was closed, so I was forced to seek food elsewhere.

That I did, and as I finished my meager nourishment I noticed a sudden glare in the sky. Since it was very close, I walked down to see whatever. "Whatever" turned out to be a three-story building almost completely enveloped in flames. A middle-aged gent was calling for help, so an older-looking Indian with whom I was gabbing and myself went down and found a couple who were attempting to salvage their belongings from the first floor. We wound up helping push and pull an antiquated oven and burners from the building. Unfortunately the fire-fighting equipment was no match for this blaze, so down went the structure. With our good deed for the day completed, my Indian friend invited me to share a drink with him at the local bar. He also advised me not to get involved in conversations as it was a segregated bar—Indians only. I wisely followed his advice as I enjoyed a drink and his company. While I did notice a few inquiring stares,

I also felt quite comfortable while in the presence of my Indian friend who appeared to be one of the regulars at this bar. The tough-looking, scar-faced female bartender was very friendly, which helped ease my tension. After my short and enjoyable visit, I politely departed as discreetly as possible. When I walked back to the motel, I found Tinker lying on its side. It seems the blacktop, softened by the heat of the day, couldn't withstand the weight of Tinker and over it went. I had neglected to place my plastic shield under the side stand.

A sound, restful sleep enabled me to get an early start toward El Paso, Texas. After an overnight visit with old friends, and with a new taillight bulb for Tinker, I headed on to Route US 180 for a pleasant ride across the salt flats and an interesting fuel stop at an isolated gas station with its lonely attendant and his German shepherd. A brief chat and on to Guadalupe Mt. National Park which sports the highest point in Texas, 8,750 feet. In this park, you will get a glimpse of El Capitan, a sheer cliff reaching 2,000 feet. Here 180 swings north and back into New Mexico, and after a short jaunt I found myself at Carlsbad Caverns.

Now, a spelunker I am not, but I couldn't resist a walk down the winding, eerie path to the bottom of this 800-foot hole in the desert floor. Naturally, with approximately fourteen acres of floor space at the bottom of this cave there is ample room for the inevitable souvenir shop, refreshment area, etc. That "etc." includes restrooms, which raises interesting questions, such as plumbing and disposal problems. After proper use of the facilities, I departed with my trivia questions unanswered. As usual it was after I returned home that I learned that those intriguing formations I viewed on the way down were "stalactites" (they hang down from the ceiling) and "stalagmites" (they rise from the floor). I also discovered that Carlsbad Caverns is one of 5,400 listed caves in the United States. How this cavern was discovered makes for very interesting perusal. The bats and the use of their droppings are all part of this intriguing story. Be sure to look it up.

Upon departing the netherworld, I found Tinker anxiously waiting to hit the road and that we did. Following US 285, by chow time, I was near Pecos, Texas. Pecos is another one of those towns that revived memories of the old western films. This town seemed to fit my image of the old cowboy films more than Yuma had, so I dallied for a nice lunch. Hunger appeased, I continued east on I-20 hoping to reach Sweetwater before darkness set in. Over the years I have found that most bikes purr along at their favorite rpm, and this Tinker's favorite was 4200 rpm. So while Tinker purred along at its favorite revs, you might say, coasting comfortably on the wings of an easterly wind, suddenly blinking lights appeared in my rearview mirror. Seems this Texas trooper had been hiding behind a bulwark, and 4200 rpm wasn't to his liking. Now 4200 rpm equals approximately seventy-five mph on this bike, but Smokey claimed eighty mph, and he was very annoyed because I was from New Jersey and that meant he would have to escort me to the local judge. He told me the judge didn't like being disturbed after dinner so he just gave me a warning ticket. I guess I upset his quota for the day, so much for Texan logic.

After this brief interruption, I spent the night in Sweetwater and with an early start headed east on I-20. A pleasant, comfortable day of excellent weather found me in Louisiana for a one night layover. From Louisiana, I-20 led me across Mississippi to the Alabama border. At this point the interstate veers in a northeasterly direction and then across Georgia to Florence, South Carolina, and I-95. There I enjoyed a nice shower, dinner, and sleep. Early next morning while feeding Tinker's tank, a young biker invited me to join him for breakfast. Usually I prefer to get a good start on the day by riding 100 to 150 miles before breakfast, but I agreed to go along with my fellow biker. About a quarter mile up the road he led me to a motel and in we went for a continental breakfast. As I sipped my second coffee, I realized this was a free repast, for guests only. I should have been suspicious when he had us park our machines out of view. I made a swift and quiet departure.

Once into Virginia, I left I-95 at Emporia and drove eastward to Rte. 58 to Norfolk. A short hop led me to the seventeen-mile Chesapeake Bay Bridge-Tunnel. This interesting route is not for one in a hurry. A relatively slow ride north on 13 and then 113 will lead you through Maryland and on to Lewes, Delaware. Lewes is the southern terminus for the Cape May Ferry. For the last hundred miles to Lewes, I had the company of a young Marine biker who was heading home to New Jersey from his base at Fort Bragg, North Carolina.

As we awaited the ferry that would carry us to Cape May, N.J., he informed me that his father worked for the ferry line. As usual, bikes were loaded and secured up front, which means first on, first off. Once our bikes were secured safely on board, we proceeded directly to the restaurant lounge for a sandwich and lots of coffee. Shortly, my buddy's father joined us for an hour-plus of chitchat. As the ferry docked, we bid farewell and then I headed north on the Garden State Parkway. Since the darkness of night had already arrived, I drove a very cautious trip, interrupted only by those annoying tollbooths.

With a midnight arrival home, and after happy greetings and a prayer of thanksgiving, I collapsed in the sack, vowing once again never to bike at night. But not before one more experience.

While perusing my book of memories, I recalled another memorable ride I enjoyed in the early eighties. I had received word that my cousin was being sent from Ireland to Houston, Texas, by the oil company that employed him. He also had vacation time available and planned to tour western Canada. We agreed to meet in Calgary, in Canada, and do the tour together. Now in my widower years I used any and all excuses to mount

Tinker and ride, ride, ride. The timing of his vacation just added more fuel to my wanderlust.

After a cross-country ride, mostly uneventful because I mostly took the interstates, I arrived in Calgary, in the province of Alberta, with a few days to spare, allowing time to treat Tinker to an oil change and minor adjustments. The plane carrying my cousin, his wife, and young daughter arrived on time, and we headed northwest, on the Trans-Canada Highway. While I rode Tinker, they followed in a rental car. Eighty miles later we took a brief look at the town of Banff, and then continued on to Lake Louise. Here we booked into a fashionable hotel and enjoyed a sumptuous dinner. Early the next morning, we went by chairlift to the top of a nearby mountain where we were awed by the view of the surrounding area as we devoured breakfast.

Lake Louise is a must on the tourist trail. It lies at an altitude of 5,680 feet, and covers an area of 1.5 by .75 miles. The lake has a depth of approximately 220 feet. The surrounding mountains with their snowcapped peaks are unbelievable. I've often heard the comment "If you have seen one mountain, you've seen them all." Well, this region disproves that thought, without challenge.

Vacation time disappears all too quickly, so now we must bid Lake Louise a farewell and ride farther north into Banff National Park, via scenic Highway 93. Along the way we experienced a sudden snow squall. We stopped to view one of the glaciers, and my cousin and daughter took the bus tour out on the ice. Of course, the bus was equipped with giant-size tires. On the road again for a short distance, and then a brief rest to enjoy the relaxing waters of the mineral hot springs.

Somewhere along the route I led them on a wrong turn, one of my rare perfections. Fifty miles later we discovered my error, but the awesome scenery made it worth the extra time, and we did get to see Canada's Glacier National Park. (Don't confuse it with the park of the same name in Montana in the US.)

Banff National Park, with its hot springs, ice fields and glaciers, covers 150 square miles. At the time of our visit, I did not know the names of the attractions we had enjoyed, but later learned we had viewed the Athabasca and Victoria glaciers and the more stable Columbia Ice-Field Cline.

As time was running out, we were forced to forgo our original goal, Jasper National Park. I did manage to lead us back to Calgary, with no wrong turns. A temporary good-bye was all that was necessary, since I intended to visit my relatives at their temporary home in Houston, on my journey home

From Calgary to Houston is approximately 2,600 miles. Rte. 2 led me south to Rte. 3, beginning with a short drive into Lethbridge, Alberta. After feeding Tinker and myself, I switched to 4 South, until I connected to I-15, which I followed into Great Falls, Montana. After an overnight visit with friends, I continued south through Wyoming and into Colorado. Somewhere in Colorado, I departed the boring interstates and found Rte. 258. Now the Interstate Highway System is great, and it does attract most of the cars and trucks, leaving the more interesting secondary roads to us bikers. I followed 285 South and after a few days found myself in Pecos, Texas, where I enjoyed a welcome night's rest.

The next morning near Fort Stockton, while having breakfast, I was given a brief insight to the history of this town, so I decided to visit. Fort Stockton was designed as a fort, and I followed the directional arrows that steered me through the entire fort. The site included original and reconstructed buildings, officers' row, guardhouse, enlisted men's barracks, and parade grounds. Added to all this is a museum and visitor center. In 1867, the 9th Cavalry returned to the fort with a new regiment created for black men, who sought security in the U.S. Army after the Civil War. They were named "Buffalo Soldiers" by the Indians.

After this brief intrusion into Texas history, I departed, with many unanswered questions, such as why the fort was built in the first place, and why it was named after Stockton, a naval officer. (He was notable for his efforts in the Mexican War.) Continuing on Route I-10 for approximately 300 hundred miles, I reached the San Antonio area. I remembered the Alamo, and my map indicated it was only a short distance from I-10, so I made my exit where I felt best. As I completed the exit, I spied a gent standing near the road, so I stopped and inquired as to the shortest route to the Alamo. With a broad smile and a bear hug greeting, this genial Tex-Mex advised, "turn right at the next corner, and go three lights, and then go left." I thanked him, and as I mounted Tinker, he waved frantically and shouted, "But don't count the first one." His amended instructions were perfect, and I arrived at the Alamo Mission. The present mission is preserved as a state park, and is located in front of the old fort, a monument to the 180-plus heroes who died there.

I have now been on the road for three weeks, and it's time to head for my Houston visit, and then home. Remember, at this time I was semiretired and a widower, so my time was pretty much my own. From San Antonio to Houston is approximately 200 miles via the interstate, I-10. In Houston, I found the temporary home of my cousin after one or two wrong turns. A two-day stay ended all too briefly. From Houston, my relatives would be in Washington, D.C., for a short stay, and I planned to visit them there too, for a final get-together before their return to Erin.

The past weeks were so enjoyable: The scenery of newfound wonders, the company of my relatives, and the off-highway routes all more than compensated for the last leg home via the monotonous interstates.

Most ruminations or reflections bring to mind interesting trails and sites I have experienced, but just as interesting are the people I have met along the way, many of whom left an indelible mark in my memories. I hesitate to name names, but I will attempt to describe a few who have left their mark.

I had one friend with whom I played golf, usually twice per week, and after golf we would mount our bikes and tour the local back roads. He later opened his own motorcycle shop in Arizona. Another friend operated a photography shop (with dried fruits as a sideline) in Prospect Park, N.J. I will call him Saul. He supplied me with my photographic needs and many evenings of chitchat, often also with the company of another friend, a minister. The rev rode a BMW similar to mine and we enjoyed many short rides together. Our chitchat in the shop often drifted into the religious area as we depleted Saul's stock of dried fruit. As a Catholic, I did gain a greater appreciation of other faiths. Saul was of the Jewish faith and the rev was a Dutch Reformed minister.

The next person to leave a deep impression was a Catholic monsignor. As a priest and biker, he reached out to all, in a variety of ways. He formed a motorcycle club in his own parish, in Paterson, N.J., and his annual "Blessing of the Motorcycles" Mass, extended an open invitation to all. Father experienced a religious retreat in the Sahara Desert, and after returning, authored an impressive book, titled "The Desert: A Rendezvous with God."

On my later Tunisian tour, my roommate would be a minster from Minnesota. This reverend had a knowledge of the Arabic language, which proved helpful on more than a few occasions. But I treasured more his presence and the many happy memories of our association.

In Panama, the Rev. Fred McTiernan took me under his wing and guided me through the final days of my Central American tour. We remained in contact until his passing.

And last, but certainly not least, the lieutenant in the Canton (Ohio) Police Department. We traveled from Alaska to Seattle together, and then eastward till we parted, in Montana. Since our meeting in the year 1978, to the present, we have remained in contact. Although not a clergyman, his thoughts and words could qualify him as one, in any faith. I thank him for the comradeship, and for augmenting my faith.

The good Lord must have felt I was in need of spiritual and worldly help. Otherwise, why did He send me such wonderful contacts?

V.
Alaska

Most, if not all, serious bikers secretly dream of attaining two goals: One, a thousand-mile day, and Two, conquer the Alcan Highway. The first dream is comparatively easy with the help of the great Interstate Highway System in the United States. Simply a matter of staying awake and ducking the four-wheelers. The second dream, a bit more elusive, is fifteen hundred miles of dirt, gravel, and slippery mud.

I had a third dream, to ride the road NEWS. That is, drive as far North, East, West, and South as the road could take me. (Bridges, tunnels, etc.—OK. But no ferries such as that from Panama to Colombia.)

Since I had previously completed a ride through Nova Scotia to its easternmost point beyond Halifax, a small town called Sydney, I had completed the E of NEWS.

My trip to Panama had taken me to the southernmost extension of road—below Panama City, near the Darien Gap, completing the S of NEWS. The Alaskan trek completed the N and W of NEWS. When I rode north beyond Fairbanks, I completed the N. Please note that the pipeline road was not open to public travel at that time (1977). After visiting Anchorage and on to Homer, the W of NEWS was accomplished. Now, I just know some kind soul will find a charming little dirt road to reach a few miles farther in all directions. Incidentally, when you reach Anchorage or Homer you are approximately 250 miles east of Hawaii (and a wee bit cooler).

On my trip to Alaska, 5,000 miles of unfamiliar roads stretched out before me, so I carefully selected my necessary tools and equipment. My travel kit included spare parts such as plugs, tubes, patch kits, pup tent, rain gear, cold-water detergent, mosquito repellent, and a very limited supply of clothes.

In what had by now gotten to be a family tradition, my aforementioned large and raucous collection of kinfolk tendered a large and raucous send-off party. Unlike my Panama venture, I refused to delay my start, and so, as my head slowly cleared, at 11:00 a.m., August 12, Tinker and I hit the road. In order to make up time and get back on schedule I drove through the night. About 3:00 a.m. the next morning found me gabbing with a toll collector some place around Chicago. It was a lonely time for him, me, and I guess, Tinker.

At high noon on Aug. 13, after almost falling asleep while tooling down the highway, I found a motel on the outskirts of St. Cloud, Minnesota. Having covered 1,243 miles in one twenty-four-hour period, I fulfilled Dream No. 1, a one-thousand-mile day. A very foolish, very unsafe dream—forget it. After receiving my key and piece of wooden shingle, I collapsed for about forever, "forever" being six hours. In the heat of summer, the parking lot macadam softens and the weight of Tinker (800 lbs.) would force the center or side stand through the softened tar and tip the bike (thus the shingle). Of course, I carried my own plastic as part of my gear, for the same purpose.

While devouring my dinner of basket chicken at a local bar, I was invited to join a few locals in a game of lotto for drinks. Well, you know the story: I was taken. After four numbers were called, one guy says "lotto." I said, "Whoa. How come?" and he says he had two T's and I said I had two O's. But you didn't call "Lotto!" says he. So I ordered the drinks and then they told me I was put on and since I was a good sport they bought the drinks. Did I have a choice? I spent an hour enjoying their company and then retired.

Good roads and light traffic made for an easy 500-mile day. En route, I had lunch at Winnipeg, Manitoba, with a couple from Hamilton, Ontario. They were traveling across Canada on a Honda Gold Wing, similar to my bike. They had left Hamilton, on the shores of Lake Ontario, picked up the Trans-Canada Highway, and planned to follow it to the end at Vancouver. Actually this highway originates in St. John's on the island of Newfoundland. As a solo biker I was often asked to join fellow bikers for lunch or dinner, as was the case here. At this time, by the way, a surge of encephalitis cases in the Winnipeg area, caused by those pesky mosquitoes, necessitated spraying via DC3s. My nice comfortable day ended at Brandon, also in the province of Manitoba.

An early departure from Brandon sent me in the direction of Regina, a beautiful, clean city and also the provincial capital of Saskatchewan. Here I left the Trans-Canada Highway and drove north to Saskatoon. I waited out a thunderstorm at a cycle shop. I did need an oil change, but they were busy, so they permitted me to use their equipment and facility to do the job myself. Between showers, I hit the road toward Lloydminster, on the border with Alberta. As my direction settled into a more northern one the scenery became more interesting. The 540 miles from Lloydminster to Dawson Creek offered generally level plains with an abundance of wheat fields, but no sizeable mountains to speak of. Plenty of dusty roads with little traffic, and I finally reached Dawson Creek about 4 p.m.

Now, Dawson Creek, a quiet town amid the rolling hills and flat plains of eastern British Columbia, is noted as the starting point, the launching pad if you will, for the Alcan Highway, said highway being the only land connection between Alaska and the United States. Since it was late in the day, I booked into an efficiency motel, and bought milk and peanuts to complement the motel's supply of Sanka. Most travelers, upon arrival, have their picture taken in front of the Mile Zero Monument, which denotes the starting point of this infamous highway. I accommodated a group of four men who were traveling by auto, and they in turn clicked my picture, all for the record. They were celebrating quite earnestly, and I never did see them again. After the picture-taking session, hot shower, and laundry duty, I hit the sack, completely forgetting the milk, peanuts, and Sanka.

Wednesday, August 17, bright and early, I was ready to attack the Alcan. Had a nice, quiet breakfast as I waited for another thunderstorm to pass. Plenty of time to ask myself, "What am I doing here?" Since I was talking to a "non compos mentis" motorcyclist, I got no reply, so I mounted Tinker and headed north. Once out of town, the dirt-and- gravel road was dusty beyond description, but when they water it, it's so slippery you can hardly stay upright, making for slow and tiresome riding. I found that ten miles per hour was the appropriate setting for Tinker, while traversing the watered sections. From Dawson Creek, I passed through Fort St. John and on to Fort Nelson. The scenery between Fort Nelson and Watson Falls was more attractive than the earlier miles. At Summit Lake Pass, you reach the highest altitude on the Alcan, 1,295 feet. While you can see higher elevations off in the distance, the almost level road follows a river at every opportunity, in this area the Tetsa River. From this point on, I resolved to take it easy as you just can't make time on this trail (I refuse to call it a highway). En route to Summit Lake, I experienced my first taste of slippery mud. It seems the road crews soak five-mile segments with a mixture of water and alkali. The calcium in the mixture holds the mud together and graders then level the surface. You can expect these slippery segments about every 100 miles in summer.

After leaving Summit Lake the dusty trail wasn't too bad, and I continued along the not-too-exciting scenery toward Watson Lake. My electric start switch gave out and for the balance of the day I had to use the kick start to rev up Tinker. At Watson Lake I found a would-be mechanic who attempted to repair it. After one hour and a six-pack of Bud, midst a shower of sparks, the starter came to life. Since it was getting late, I stayed the night and enjoyed the live country music while I supped. Motel prices are increasing as I travel north.

Watson Lake, the first town you reach in the Yukon Territory, is famous for its unique signpost. In 1942, a homesick GI, working on the construction of the Alcan Highway, erected a sign showing the mileage to his hometown. This started a trend. Other GIs followed suit, and after WWII, tourists continued the trend by planting signs, usually lifted from their hometowns. Reminiscent of the ETO scribbling "Kilroy was here."[7]

After a few photos for the record, I departed Watson Lake. Miles and miles of dust and gravel. Then, as I approached the crest of a mild rise, I spied a large moose in the road. Naturally I stopped and set my telescopic lens in place to snap a few pics. As the cow moose and her calf ambled off into the marsh, I felt I could ride down and click a few more shots at a safe distance. No sane person argues with any wild animal—especially one protecting her offspring. Returning to Tinker, I was amazed to see a pack of at least twenty large animals ambling roadside. They passed me close enough to touch. Turned out to be a breed of goat, about shoulder high to me. They ignored me and my clicking camera completely. After approximately 450 miles, I reached the fair-sized city of Whitehorse, population then about 15,000 and the

---

7   During WWII, even when you thought your outfit was first to secure some small German town, somewhere you could find the scribble "Kilroy was here."

territorial capital. Now Tinker had new rubber, front and rear, when I left Jersey, and normally I expect six to eight thousand miles out of a rear tire, but here I am with a balding tire at only four thousand miles, due to the wear and tear of the gravel. I canvassed Whitehorse for a tire but the best they could do was fly one in by the next day. I opted to chance it with what I had.

Since I was anxious to move on, I gave Whitehorse a cursory inspection and rode off on relatively good gravel until I caught up to a graded area. Traveling about 5 to 10 mph through the five-inch-deep slippery mud, I suddenly found myself and Tinker lying in the ooze.

Seems the mud had built up twixt the fender and front wheel, which in turn locked the wheel, and over we went. After righting the bike and removing the caked mud, I started the engine, but oil came squirting out from a ruptured valve cover. My only choice was to push Tinker off the road into the drainage ditch and wait for help. So much for the slogan "Good things happen on a Honda." Close to a half hour passed, when along came a kindly Indian couple in a not-so-new station wagon.

Of course they stopped, and of course I accepted their offer of aid, and promptly loaded my tank bag containing my camera goods and off we went for a fifty-mile lift before we reached a gas station. My benefactor continued on after my profuse thanks. All gas stations on the Alcan keep a van and/or tow truck ready for disabled travelers. These service stops are definitely not, even remotely, similar to their counterpart on the interstates. A service station on this highway means a garage with gas pumps, owner mechanic, tow truck, and emergency repairs. One beautiful feature of the Alcan is the friendly and helpful attitude of total strangers to each other. No one would ever think of passing a stranded fellow human. It reminds us older folks how people helped each other during the Great Depression and other troubled times.

After explaining my predicament, the operator of this station directed his young helper to head back and fetch Tinker. Since I had noted the mile marker closest to where I had left wounded Tinker, we had no trouble locating it. A mile marker is a very important item along this trail for many reasons. Back in Dawson Creek I purchased a small booklet, aptly named "Mile Marker." This informative booklet tells you the location of whatever you may be looking for, whether it be a motel, gas station, food shop, or whatever. At $.95 it was not only a bargain, but a necessity. To fit Tinker into the van, we removed the fairing and saddlebags. It was a very hot afternoon, so on the return trip we quenched our thirst with a cool drink, direct from a flowing stream with no fear of pollution.

Back at the garage the first question asked by the owner was "Why do you bikers do this to yourselves?" My answer was "Please tell *me* so I won't do it again." As he worked at patching the punctured valve cover with fender putty, I reassembled Tinker. Since the day was waning, he invited me to sleep in his garage but I opted for my pup tent and bedroll, as opposed to the cement floor.

As with most stops along the Alcan, proprietors protect their property with guard dogs. This stop was no exception and had a sort-of-friendly German shepherd and a pup Doberman pinscher. The pup was kept tied up to make him nasty as the owner felt the shepherd was too friendly. Protection is needed to ward off stupid night travelers, some of whom feel no compunction about borrowing a few gallons of gas from unattended pumps.

After crawling into my sack and drifting off to dreamland, I suddenly realized I had company. Seems our shepherd friend needed to keep an eye on me, or desired the warmth of my body and tent, and at this point only a fool would argue with a German shepherd. As dawn broke, I awoke, and my canine friend ran out and angrily chased a would-be customer back into his car. The owner promptly filled his tank and sent him safely on his way, as he muttered unkindly words at the protective shepherd.

With my gear packed securely aboard, I bid my hospitable benefactor farewell and rode off in the direction of Haines Junction. This being Saturday, the work crews were off for the weekend, so I pressed forward happy with the absence of slick mud, and only the dust to contend with. Whenever I spied a cloud of dust in the distance, I would stop and allow the inevitable logging truck to rumble by amidst a shower of dust, stones, and cinders. Of course, like most Alcan travelers I had covered my headlight with mesh wire to preserve the lens. Many cars had their headlights, radiator, and windshield covered. In Haines Junction I stopped and enjoyed my first food in twenty-four hours. At the junction you have a choice—continue on to Fairbanks or take the cut-off to Haines City, about two hundred miles distant, where you can board the ferry for Seattle and home. I heard of travelers, exhausted from the rigors of the Alcan, who opted for the latter. I continued toward Fairbanks and, while clearing the Alaskan border to re-enter the USA, a Greyhound driver clued me in on what to be wary of. In Alaska the main roads are paved, but after suffering the ravages of winter there were more than a few areas in need of repair. These pop up unexpectedly, and are covered with crushed, sharp stones, which could be disastrous to my very worn rear tire. I survived these areas with slow speed and quick prayers. My weekend ended at Tok Junction, where I booked into a motel managed by a young fellow from Philadelphia. Being almost neighbors, we had a nice chat over a few drinks. I gathered he was a wee bit homesick, and I being a lonesome biker, conversation flowed freely and all too briefly. I sacked out looking forward to the final leg of my trek to the fair city of Fairbanks.

Day by day the scenery becomes more and more exciting, and day by day the cost of food and motels rises. While the food was expensive, the portions were massive. The relatively short ride to Fairbanks was completed shortly before noon—the farthest point of my bike journey, the journey to the end, Alaska. Alone with the great mountains, the valleys, the animals, the tundra, alone with nature, alone with God. I registered at a hotel whose only inducement was its proximity to a Honda shop. I was shocked by the hotel's charge of $41, single (1977, remember). You may have realized (at least, you won't be surprised) that I was riding a 1,000cc 1975 Honda Gold Wing. This was Honda's first venture into the 1,000cc engine class.

I made a brief, self-escorted tour of Fairbanks, a not-too-large city of approximately 20,000 population, located less than one hundred miles south of the Arctic Circle. Fairbanks has experienced winter temperatures as low as minus 60 degrees Fahrenheit and summer temps as high as 90. I dined at Kentucky Fried Chicken. As usual, the serving was so large I couldn't finish it. The people with whom I came in contact on this journey, from start to finish, have been most friendly and helpful. I think people in general feel intimidated by groups of bikers, but as a loner they felt free to converse, and inquire about Tinker and our travels.

My first order of business in Fairbanks was to move out of the hotel. I had no choice as the hotel was expecting a tour group from Europe and said tour had booked the entire hotel. Plus it was just too expensive for my budget. So off I went to a campground at five dollars per day, public shower included. The second order of business was to deliver Tinker to the Honda shop for new rubber and a badly needed checkup. I missed Tinker but my gluteus maximus[8] did need a rest. Then, via taxi, I headed for the airport and boarded a six-passenger plane for a flight over the Arctic Circle to Fort Yukon. It was a bumpy ride over the pipeline, with spectacular views of mountains peaks that seem to poke at the clouds. The mountains were interrupted only by the equally impressive valleys. En route I enjoyed the company of two telephone engineers who were installing phone service, via satellite, from Fort Yukon to the rest of us. You see, this is not an

---

8   The part of the human anatomy we use to sit on, commonly called the "ass" or "keister." *Tóin* for Irish types.

area for telephone poles and wires. The other two passengers were an interesting and dedicated husband-wife teacher team on their way to aid the school program in Ft. Yukon.

As part of my Fort Yukon tour, a yellow school bus met me at the small airstrip. Picture this, if you will—a tour consisting of one tourist, a school bus, and a sixteen-year-old Athabascan Indian lassie as the driver guide. All this for a very isolated town of six hundred. The tour included a visit to the old fort, which was in a state of reconstruction, salmon traps, sleds, and huskies tied up separately to avoid conflict. Homes were of the log cabin type, and some exhibited a slight tilt due to construction that doesn't quite accommodate the permafrost. The last stop of the tour was the local interpretation of a supermarket, with the hope that you will spend a few bucks on items you don't need. I cooperated. The natives hunt, fish, and trap for survival. A few cars and bikes are used when possible. Fort Yukon at one time held the extreme temperature record of the US: a low of minus seventy-eight degrees and a high of one hundred degrees Fahrenheit.

The young tour guide was very well versed in the lore of the land and people, and she made my all-too-short stay extremely interesting and educational. She earned $1,000 per month (1977). The poverty level in Alaska at this time was $11,000 per annum. Practically all residents of Fort Yukon are Athabascan Indians, also known as Athapaskans or Denes. Their language is related to those used by the tribes in the Yukon Basin and other parts of Alaska, and by the Navajos in Arizona. I was told that researchers are studying the link between the Navajos and their Arctic counterparts.

Because of the dedicated efforts of Presbyterian missionaries, most inhabitants are of this faith. Their church, worthy of any denomination, displayed some truly artistic bead- and needlework in the altar linens. As if any further proof was needed to show the talents and artistic ability of the Indians here. While Fort Yukon is not exactly a tourist mecca, I felt it was a worthwhile visit. As I've said many times, "tourists travel to view the sights, while travelers travel to visit the people." It was a Presbyterian missionary, the Rev. Sheldon Jackson, by the way, who introduced reindeer to Alaska in an effort to aid the Eskimos.

The return flight to Fairbanks offered a second chance to view the wondrous mountains separated by the equally wondrous valleys. The same cab driver that had dropped me off earlier had agreed to meet me upon my return, and there he was. He was accompanied by his wife and they very kindly invited me to join them for dinner. I felt I had inconvenienced them enough with my late arrival, and the wait for my certificate attesting that I had crossed the Arctic Circle, so I declined. And so, without any New York City surcharge, he delivered me to my campground. After a nice shower I ambled over to Alaska Land, a sort of undersized theme-park, for a gourmet dinner consisting of a one-foot-long hot dog washed down by an ample supply of beer. I ended this wonderful day with a visit to the River Boat and listened to the tinkly piano. Great entertainment, but few customers.

Following a good night sleep in my private pup tent, my friendly cabby drove me to the Honda shop to retrieve Tinker, but old Tinker was in need of shocks, so I added them to my shopping list for Anchorage. We then taxied to the train station with minutes to spare. The eleven-hour train ride, Fairbanks to Anchorage, was made bearable by the spectacular scenery and the club car. At Denali Park the train halted for a picture-taking session. Mt. McKinley (Denali), at twenty thousand feet, is easily the highest peak in North America, and just awesome. Because of the clouds and general weather conditions, a clear view is possible only a few weeks per year. To pass the time, I checked out the lounge car, vista dome, etc. I was shocked to see so many people nursing hard drinks and beer the entire trip. Food and drink were very expensive on the train, as they were throughout Alaska. The pay scale is also very high. As the train dieseled on through the scenic valleys and hills, following riverbeds here and there, traversing scary trestles at slow speed, I found myself engrossed in Alaska trivia—like the state flag. It seems the Alaskan territorial flag was designed by a thirteen-year old, an Aleut boy named Benny Benson, who received one thousand dollars for his winning entry. It was adopted in 1927. After statehood, in 1959, Alaska adopted it for state use. The blue field equals the sky, the sea, and mountain lakes, as well as Alaska's wild flowers. Seven of the flag's eight stars represent Ursa Major ("great bear") or more commonly, the Big Dipper, and the eighth the North Star, standing for Alaska itself, the northernmost state. This is from the mind of a very bright thirteen-year-old. I also discovered that the distance from Attu, Alaska's most westward island, to Ketchikan, in the panhandle, is greater than the distance from San Francisco to New York.

After eleven hours of monotonous clickity-clack, interrupted by periods of exciting scenery, we crept into the Anchorage terminal, headquarters for the Alaskan railroad. With wide streets and many new buildings it's difficult to picture the devastation of the 1964 earthquake. Anchorage, located farther north than Helsinki, Finland, is blessed with a surprisingly moderate climate, no doubt due to the influence of the warm ocean currents. About fifty miles northeast of Anchorage lies the Matanuska Valley along the Susitna River and extending eastward. Now people don't often think of Alaska as an agricultural state, but this fertile valley produces a variety of monster-size veggies, such as potatoes, carrots, and cabbages. One prize-winning cabbage weighed in at forty-plus pounds. Turnips have tipped the scales at approximately thirty pounds. This is the result of the rich fertile soil, the many hours of sunshine in the summer, and just the right amount of soft rain.

The Holiday Inn in Anchorage was fairly close to the rail station and it provided a nice, clean room. I was still not accustomed to the high cost of living here, but at least I wasn't shocked anymore.

With a good night's sleep and a hearty breakfast behind me, I taxied to the Honda shop and purchased a rear grip, shocks, and valve cover, at a cost of $75. Checked with a travel agent and found I could fly back to Fairbanks for forty-two dollars, so I took a refund of twenty-seven dollars on my train ticket and headed for the airport. Plane takes about one hour plus, as opposed to eleven hours by train. If I get back to the campground early and get Tinker ready, I'll try to make the Haines morning ferry. As I flew out of Anchorage, I experienced my first cloudy day in Alaska, but as we headed for Fairbanks it cleared. Once again I had an excellent view of Mt. McKinley. After deplaning I headed for the local Honda and with the generous help of the operator I installed the rear grip and shocks. Since the fender putty repair still looked good, I left it as is. Then back to the campground to gather my gear and check out. The camp Boss Lady remarked that she hadn't seen me, and when I told her where I had been (Fort Yukon, Anchorage, etc.), she decided, since I had slept there only one or two nights, that she would charge me for one night. The Honda dealer, taxi driver, and camp owner, these wonderful people, provided me with many long-lasting and pleasant memories. While my memories of the great state of Alaska may begin to fade, my memories of the people I met along my journey will last forever.

Before departing Fairbanks, I mapped out my itinerary for the return trip. I planned to briefly leave Alaska via the Alcan Highway into Canada, then continue southward to Haines Junction, at this point leaving the Alcan onto Rte. 3, the Haines Highway. This highway (or trail), after a few hundred miles of gravel and mud, leads into the Alaskan panhandle and the city of Haines. Here I planned to board the Alaskan ferry, which comes down from Skagway, and hopefully, after three days would deliver me and Tinker to Vancouver or Seattle. Then the eastward trek via Montana and South Dakota, and routes 90 and 80 to home.

I finally left the campground at six p.m. and by eleven, reached the village of Tok, which very conveniently had a gas station and inn available. I availed myself of both. With my face shield covered by bugs and my weary bones chilled by the cold evening air, no way could I hope to reach the ferry by morning. I had a very welcome bowl of soup and some hot coffee, and flopped those same weary bones into the sack.

Five a.m. found me scraping ice off Tinker's saddle and packing my gear. One hundred fifty miles down the Alaskan macadam I reached the Canadian border and the dust, gravel, and mud. I caught up to the infernal water trucks so I laid up for two hours, but it didn't help as the mud was still wet, slippery, and deep. Another hundred miles, and déja vu. Five to ten miles per hour is about the best you can do for the five or six miles of slop. With one hundred sixty miles still before me when I arrived at Haines Junction at seven p.m., I took a room, shower, soup and sandwich, and sacked out. (Alaskan soup is more like a stew and as filling as a full dinner.) The going is slow and exhausting, which adds up to a sound sleep. My original dream of leaving Fairbanks at six p.m. and making the six- hundred-mile-distant ferry by morning, was just that, a dream. So I missed the ferry to Vancouver by only two days, but I still had a chance to make the ferry to Seattle on Aug. 28. As you can see, my planned overnight trip to the ferry turned out to be a three-day struggle. Just goes to show you what a tired brain, tired body, and worn-out bike can do for you.

On the road again at eight a.m., Aug. 26, and—you guessed it—I caught up to those damn water trucks again. This time, I followed the grader for approximately eight miles at its usual five mph, but at least the grader provided a fairly level, if slippery, ride. At Kathleen Lake, a very scenic area on the Haines Highway, I stopped for breakfast. While chatting with a ranger he advised me to be alert for a small grizzly that was foraging the local garbage pails. The rangers planned to tranquilize it and transfer Little

Bear to the deep wilds. Attacks by bears are not too common, but the danger is ever present. Just a few days before, a female survey-crew member had been badly mauled by a brown bear, which was finally scared off by a helicopter.

While gassing up Tinker, the female attendant and I engaged in world-shattering chitchat. I almost fell over when she very seriously asked if I would take her and her pet German shepherd to the Lower 48 on my bike. She desperately desired to leave this desolate area and settle in the lower states. I gently explained that Tinker was not designed to carry such cargo and hurried off. All my complaints about water trucks and road conditions faded into insignificance as I viewed the scenic wonders of the Wrangell Mountains, with numerous snowcapped, 12,000-foot peaks. Mt. St. Elias, at 18,000 feet, is also spectacular. The Haines Highway follows the southern slopes, more accurately the eastern aspect, offering a pretty level ride into the city of Haines, after once again crossing the Canadian border back into Alaska.

Haines is (or was) a real frontier town, sporting the usual attractions, such as bars with their locals bragging about their previous night's fights and escapades, restaurants, and a ferry terminal. Bought a ticket to Seattle and then found a pretty nice room, took care of the usual chores, and had dinner. Took a walking tour about town, all six blocks, to work up an appetite for a couple beers before sack time.

At last, it was Saturday, Aug. 27, what they call in the carnival "get away day." I was up early and took a few photos and checked out the old hotel on a distant hill. Said hotel was formerly headquarters for General Seward. Of course, you remember him of Seward's Folly fame. The purchase of Alaska for eight million dollars was quite a buy. Imagine all this for roughly two cents an acre: five hundred eighty-six thousand square miles of mountains, plains, trees, mosses and lichen, tundra, rivers, lakes, sand dunes. The tundra, frozen plains, is frozen to depths of one thousand feet. Alaska's coastline is longer than the Lower 48's Atlantic and

Pacific coasts combined. It is two and one-half times the size of Texas, nine times the size of New England, and equals twenty percent of the entire rest of the country. Among the numerous glaciers, the Malaspina equals the size of Rhode Island. Over one half the lakes in the United States are in Alaska. Plus a plentiful supply of precious and nonprecious metals, including gold, silver, copper, platinum, and mercury. Add to this oil reserves that stretch the imagination, but more about that later.

I arrived at the ferry terminal pretty early and learned that Tinker would have the company of another bike on our boat ride. Excuse me—ship. Seems our crew prefers to call it a ship. As usual motorcycles were placed at the front of the line to facilitate loading. Since the ship carries hundreds of vehicles, including trailer trucks and cars of all design, the bikes are usually tied up to posts, etc. with an eye to stability (Tinker has only two wheels, remember). As the other biker awakened from his wooden bench nap we introduced ourselves. He was the police lieutenant from Canton, Ohio. The beginning of a lifelong friendship.

The ferry, the *Malaspina* (probably named after the Malaspina Glacier, which in turn probably was named after somebody, and so on) arrived from Skagway on time. Skagway is the northern terminus of the Alaskan ferry. It connects by highway with the Yukon Territory of Canada and is famous as a stop along the way there during the gold rush days. Eventually a narrow-gauge railroad was built to Whitehorse. It's still a popular attraction. In that era came some who struck it rich, many who went broke, but all leaving an abundance of colorful stories and equally colorful names. Throughout the Yukon Territory and Alaska I came across such names as Skagway Kate, Crooked Leg Louie, Moosehide Annie, Malamute Kid, and Snuffbox Olsen.

But now back to the ferry. Vehicles and passengers were loaded without delay, and it then sailed down the Inland Passage toward our first stop, Juneau, the capital city of Alaska. Sixteen hundred miles north of Seattle, Juneau enjoys a very mild, although rather damp, climate. From the ship, the city looks like a stage, with Mt. Robert and Mt. Juneau as a backdrop that rises to a height of 3,500 feet. Forty miles north of the capital is the Mendenhall Glacier. Juneau can be reached only by air or sea, but since the harbor is ice-free year round, it offers easy accessibility. It took its name from Joe Juneau, who with Richard Harris discovered gold in the area in 1880. In 1976 it was voted to move the capital to a site north of Anchorage, but in 1982 voters decided to retain Juneau.

Just about the entire panhandle of Alaska lies within the Tongas National Forest with its abundance of bald eagles and a variety of smaller birds, and of course all kinds of animals, big and small. Alaska, including the panhandle, provides a welcome environment for nine kinds of salmon, trout, crabs up to five feet wide and weighing up to twenty-six pounds, whales up to forty tons and fifty feet long. Brown and black bears (grizzly, or brown, bears need 100 square miles to survive), bald eagles, Dall sheep, fox, wolves, deer, elk, antelope, caribou, moose, goats, sea lions, sea otters, walrus, polar bears, and musk oxen. It would be easier to list those not found in Alaska. Did I forget beavers, woodchucks, squirrels, and the rabbitlike pikas? And never forget the numerous pesky mosquitoes.

Excuse me, I keep wandering! Our stop at Juneau was actually shorter than my verbose description. After unloading a few trucks, cars, and passengers, and taking on a few trucks, cars, and passengers, we sailed on toward Sitka. As if the scenery wasn't enough to keep us occupied, the ship provided a bar, restaurant, and lounge. Also three movies per day, plus two lectures. Both films and lectures were extremely interesting and I found myself looking forward to the next session. In three days aboard, I learned more about Alaska and its history than I ever did in twenty-plus years of formal schooling.

The solarium, on the upper deck of the aft section of the ship, was mainly occupied by the younger set, backpackers, and van travelers. The lieutenant and I paid a visit to the solarium to see how our fellow passengers were faring. One shaggy-haired juggler displayed his talents with the help of three oranges while another would-be saxophonist filled the air with his not too melodic efforts. We gave them each an A for effort. The sweet essence of hemp permeated the atmosphere. I had put my name on standby for a room and I was offered a cabin if I would share it. My roommate turned out to be an engineer who had just completed his work on the pipeline project and was on his way from Prudhoe Bay to Saudi Arabia. The cabin had four bunks, private shower, and a small version of a picture window.

Evenings we sat in the cafeteria—the lieutenant, the engineer, a math professor from Berkeley, and I—and gabbed. Often we invited young fellows to join us so we could pick their brains. Most of the serious ones went to Alaska to work as fishermen or in logging camps, taking advantage of the high pay scale for a few years in order to return home in the Lower 48 and set up a small business. Assuming, of course, they survived the hazards of these very dangerous occupations. After Sitka, the ship sailed south to Petersburg and as I awoke on Sunday, August 28, we were docking at Wrangell. All the stops were relatively short, so at each one I scrambled up on deck, camera in hand. These settlements are unbelievably picturesque, if a little desolate. Make that *very* desolate.

While in our stateroom, my engineer friend filled me in on some pipeline data. Now if the pipeline doesn't grab you, please skip this paragraph. The 800-mile pipe cost $7.7 billion dollars, and was (or is) owned by Sohio (53%), which is owned by British Petroleum. The carbon steel pipe was made by Japan. It is 48 inches in diameter, with three-inch walls insulated by plastic liner of similar thickness. Oil enters the pipe at 135 degrees Fahrenheit and the friction of the flowing oil keeps the temperature above 100 degrees. About 400 miles of pipe are above ground and, since the supporting uprights are set into the permafrost, they must be refrigerated to prevent thawing. The line has nine pumping stations to maintain the flow, and reaches elevations of up to 4,700 feet, while at other points it is under the ground. It sways up to 20 feet and has ups and downs of five feet. Oil reserves were estimated to be a twenty-year supply at two million barrels of crude per day.

The light rain kept us inside as the ship slipped into Ketchikan, a fairly large settlement overflowing with small planes and boats. Understandable, since these are the only ways to reach this fine city. Its claim to fame as the wettest city in the United States, with 150 inches of rain per year, was short-lived. The dubious honor was lost when Hawaii entered the Union in August 1959, with an annual rainfall that easily topped the Ketchikan record. (Alaska entered in January 1959.)

After Ketchikan the sea was quite rough, but the weather cleared and I was happy that this was our last day on the water—a sailor, I am not. Suddenly, I fully realized we were actually leaving Alaska, Alaska with its indescribable beauty. I could only repeat Psalm 9:2 — "I will praise You, Lord, with all my heart: I will declare all Your wondrous deeds." Of course our regular gang (by now we were almost family), gabbed our way well past midnight and, since the schedule called for early a.m. docking, we exchanged addresses and promises to keep in touch, knowing full well we wouldn't.

A heavy five-thirty a.m. knock on the cabin door ended my peaceful five-hour slumber. Peeking out my picture window, I enjoyed a welcome view of Seattle as the *Malaspina* docked. Had time for a quick cup of coffee before going below to prepare Tinker for the next leg of the homeward trek. Because my bike was anchored near the exit, I rolled off among the first group to debark and waited on the pier for my lieutenant buddy. Before we departed, a couple we had met on board stopped to take our picture and swap addresses and more promises to write.

The next thirty miles were wet ones, but as we approached the mountain pass, the weather cleared so we enjoyed a very pleasant 280-mile ride to Spokane. After three days of shipboard activity, it was great to be back on Tinker and feel the wind in my face. In Spokane, I found a cycle shop where I could purchase a windshield to replace the one fractured when I dumped Tinker on the way up. My buddy and I installed same, and we headed east enjoying the snowcapped mountain peaks and wide-open spaces, a showroom of God's handiwork.

Near Idaho we caught up with the rain again, a good excuse for a coffee stop at a quaint emporium, a combination bar and food outlet that had one wall covered with dollar bills, all autographed and donated by on-the-road visitors. Along about dusk, we reached Missoula, Montana. I decided to stay the night there, but since my riding buddy was due back on duty in a few days he continued eastward. We said our good-byes and once again promised to keep in touch. This time we meant it.

After a refreshing shower, I phoned home and then called my St. Louis U classmate who lived in my next stop, Great Falls, Montana. Why do I keep mentioning "refreshing showers"? Probably because they seem so special after two-wheeling down the roadway all day, picking up all kinds of dirt and grime.

Early morning on Aug. 31 found me heading east on a very foggy road. No traffic, but the winding trail, plus fog, dictated slow travel. As I gradually climbed to higher elevations, the fog cleared and once again I marveled at the beautiful, majestic mountains. At Rogers Pass, elevation 5,600 feet, I crossed the Continental Divide and then, on the downside, I completed the 175-mile segment to Great Falls.

My classmate and his wife greeted me with an immediate tour of the city, golf course included. We viewed the dams and waterfalls (about seven) along the Missouri River, and I was particularly impressed by the Great Springs that produce 474,000 gallons per minute. This was followed by a sumptuous cookout and a gab session that stretched into the wee hours, and I wearily flopped into bed.

Bright and early (maybe not bright but definitely early) next morning, I embarked on a six-hundred-mile jaunt to Rapid City, South Dakota. Chased by the rain all day, but my luck held out. As I exited Montana, I decided, after visiting all fifty states, that Montana has my vote for the most beautiful and scenic state in the Union. Made a brief photo stop at Big Horn and Little Big Horn Monument (remember General Custer).

It was still daylight when I tooled into Rapid City, so I checked into a motel, unloaded my gear and headed straight for Mount Rushmore. I have never been overly impressed by man-made structures, but I did snap a few photos, skipped the souvenir shops, and headed back to the motel and sleep.

Heading east out of Rapid City, the rain caught up with me on and off. I finally outran the storms and, since we were both heading in the same direction, I thought it best to drive through the night and thus keep dry. I grabbed a few short naps at roadside rest areas. Picnic benches do not make comfortable bunks. Somewhere in the Chicago area, I left Rte. 90 and picked up Rte. 80. Grabbed a few hours shut-eye in a maintenance yard that was conveniently left open—not exactly Motel 6. I didn't see a light in the window, but I dropped in anyway.

About noon the next day, I bumped into a young biker at a deserted rest area. He was busy preparing a gourmet lunch, a can of beans over a small Sterno setup, and he cordially invited me to share lunch. An invitation from the heart. I thanked him and begged off as I had just had lunch—a little white lie.

By midnight I was in Pennsylvania and ready for some slumber. Pennsy frowns on pup tents at rest areas so I used my tent for groundcover and slept for two hours. Having not seen a motel since Rapid City, So. Dakota, I was beginning to look a little grimy so I washed and shaved before exiting the rest stop.

Once again on the road and feeling refreshed, I anxiously looked for the Delaware Water Gap, the entry gate to New Jersey and home. My dreams were cut short by a new problem: About every mile, groups of deer appeared, grazing roadside. Now deer can be quite unpredictable, and motorcycles were not designed for arguments with any animal, big or small, so I opted for an early breakfast at the first available opportunity, which turned out to be a truck stop. Ugh, ugh. I sat over coffee and more coffee, as I listened to the idle gab of the truckers and waited for daylight. When at last dawn arrived, Tinker and I headed for the few remaining miles to home, while mentally trying to decide which was more rank—the coffee or the trucker's language. It is often said that getting there is half the fun. Well, I guess the other half must be arriving home, and once again being with your family, not to mention being just in time for the annual Labor Day Picnic.

Well, I arrived home in one piece about six a.m., awakened my family (hearty greetings all around), and collapsed till picnic time. Eating, drinking, and swimming for five hours put Labor Day and me to bed. A good night's sleep and a clear head led me to some reflections on the past month. My travels had included 9,000 miles on Tinker, 1,600 miles on board a ship, 700 miles via plane, and 400 miles by train, for a total of 11,700 miles.

The mileage aboard Tinker was spread amongst fourteen of our states and five Canadian provinces (counting the Yukon, which is really a territory). While the scenery, vernacular, and the people may differ, the various states and provinces offer at least one consistent pattern concerning motorcycles: Children wave to you, dogs chase you, and cars tailgate you.

VI.
El Camino
Real

One of our nation's most interesting and educational journeys follows California's El Camino Real, a 650-mile trail that stretches from San Diego to Sonora, just north of Frisco. It was along this trace that the Franciscan missionaries, led by Padre Junípero Serra, founded twenty-one missions. Nine of these were founded by Fr. Serra himself. They are spaced approximately thirty miles apart, a one-day journey in those days. You might say El Camino Real (The Royal Road) started in Veracruz, Mexico, then led to Mexico City, and then continued on to San Diego, and places farther to the north. Since this is Padre Serra's trail, you could even say it all began in Majorca, the Spanish island in the Mediterranean where he was born.

These missions helped shape the future of California. Today California is one of the agricultural giants of the US, and more than 60% of its population lives in areas around the twenty-one missions.

While performing their religious assignments, the missionaries introduced fruits, vegetables, grains, olives, and grapes to the area.

Why California? Well, Spanish missionaries were working mainly in Mexico and while their goal was to carry Christianity to the natives, the Spanish government also sent the military to lay claim to these lands. In response to territorial threats by the British and Russians, the Spaniards launched a mission development into California, accompanied of course by the military.

So why would anyone take a 6,000-mile trip on a motorcycle just to follow a 650-mile trail? Well, there are more than a few reasons why I chose to do just that. Number One, as a member of Serra International[9] since 1958, I had developed a keen interest in Serra's life. I had previously visited his birthplace in Petra, located on the island of Majorca, and now I was anxious to retrace his journey along the Camino Real and visit each of the nine missions he established.

Reason Number Two, the annual meeting of the MDA (Motorcycling Doctors Association), of which I was a past president, was scheduled for Johnson City, Tennessee, and I planned to attend said meeting as part of my return trip. North Jersey to Johnson City is only about 700 miles, but it would take me 6,400 miles to get there and thus I was later awarded the Longest Driver Award from Road Rider Magazine. A plaque and a one-year subscription to the magazine were my prizes. Reason Number Three, I wanted to relieve the stress of my daily labor: the timing just right for my annual schedule to satisfy these nomadic bones of mine for, maybe, another year.

The cross-country ride was, for the most part, on the interstates as time was an important factor. As I headed west from New Jersey, and since I arrived in Canton, Ohio, at a reasonable hour, I decided to stop at the police headquarters and pay a visit to my lieutenant friend with whom I had ridden down from Alaska in 1977. A phone call from the chief brought him

---

9   Serra International--An organization of Catholic men and women dedicated to promoting vocations to the religious life. As the name implies it is worldwide.

from home and while awaiting his arrival, I had the pleasure of meeting many of the department's motorcycle squad, this time *sans* siren and flashing lights. After a pleasant lunch at his home, with his pet ocelot safely tucked away, I departed in the direction of Columbus, Ohio, then south through Cincinnati and into Kentucky where I spent an overnight visit with dear friends from St. Louis University days. An evening of reminiscing and good cheer was followed by a sound sleep and a not so early departure. Next stop, St. Louis, with a short peek at my alma mater, and then on to Tulsa, Oklahoma, for another overnight stay, this time with my very hospitable new in-laws. I continued westward through Texas and New Mexico. In Prescott, Arizona, I made a brief visit with the old golfing buddy who operated a motorcycle agency there. And then on to San Diego, California, to pick up the mission trail.

My journey up the Camino Real started in San Diego, where Fr. Serra founded his first Californian mission. All the missions founded by Fr. Serra are located on or near what is now Rte. 101, sometimes referred to as "Fr. Serra Highway." Serra's missions were founded over a period of thirteen years, from 1769 to 1782. Surprisingly, Fray Serra traveled more than 600 miles on foot and horseback to settle his second mission. As you will see, I visited the missions in a south-to-north fashion, not in the order of their founding.

Mission San Diego Alcalá, founded in 1769, is the oldest mission in California, the initial link in the chain of twenty-one missions that stretches 650 miles up the Camino Real. This mission is a modest structure for one of such historic importance. The plain, almost homely facade lacks the elaborateness of some of its successors, but its simplicity and rough-hewn character, perhaps, reflects more the spirit of the founding padres than some of the more sophisticated structures that followed. Originally built on Presidio Hill above the old town, it was moved to the present site in 1774. It was burned by marauding Indians, rebuilt, destroyed by earthquake in 1803, restored and enlarged in 1813. It was rebuilt once again in 1831, secularized in 1834, sold in 1845 and returned to the church in 1862. This is pretty much the story of all the missions. The present church contains the usual mission museum replete with a fine collection of mission antiques. While Mission San Diego Alcalá was my reason for visiting this fine city, I found San Diego so intriguing as to add a few days to my stay. It's the oldest city in California and sports a great deepwater harbor. Much of the harbor area is occupied by military installations. Balboa Park covers more than 1,000 acres in the center of the city and includes the world-famous zoo.

A short ride north on I-5 took me to San Juan Capistrano. Actually this was the seventh mission founded by Fr. Serra, and I'm certain that everyone is familiar with the true story of the swallows returning each year, on or about March 19, St. Joseph's Feast day, to build their mud nests in the ruins of the old mission. The church is of magnificent proportions, and the most ornate of the Serran missions. With a ceiling divided into six domes, it was nine years in building. After only six years of use, it collapsed during an earthquake in 1812. The small remaining chapel is called "Fr. Serra Church" because it is the only building still standing anywhere in the mission chain in which it is known for sure that Fr. Serra actually conducted divine service.

Now heading north on I-5 to Rte. 710 to Valley Blvd., and with some good luck I found San Gabriel Arcángel, founded in 1771, and that makes it older than Los Angeles. Indeed, it was from here, ten years after the founding of the mission that a small party marched the nine miles to found "The City of Our Lady Queen of the Angels," now called Los Angeles. The old mission church with buttressed walls of stone and brick has much the appearance today as the original, except that, after the bell tower fell during an earthquake, the padre replaced it with the present campanario[10] at the opposite end of the building. Today San

10 Campanario—a bell tower that is not part of a building.

Gabriel possesses perhaps the finest collection of mission relics in existence. Its hammered copper baptismal font was a gift of King Carlos III of Spain in 1771. The six altar statues were brought around the Horn from Spain. They are priceless.

From San Gabriel Mission I found my way north to Rte. 210 and with the help of a half-dozen wrong turns I saw more of Los Angeles than I had planned or cared to see. Rte. 210 west leads back to 134 and 101 to Ventura. Now it's easy—the mission is conveniently located right on Main Street. The Mission of San Buenaventura was the third planned by Padre Serra but it was delayed because of provincial politics and Indian unrest; it turned out to be the ninth to be founded. Now located on the main street of a city, it might be difficult to imagine the old church surrounded by the orchards, vineyards, and grain fields that made it the garden spot of the missions. Like all the other missions, Buenaventura also suffered from earthquakes and fire. The museum's lack of size is inversely proportional to its great interest. It includes two wooden bells, the only ones of their type in California.

Back on 101 North for about one hundred miles, with Los Angeles safely behind us (Tinker and me), we can now enjoy a more relaxed view of the surrounding scenery. Sometimes, in our anxiety to get where we are going we forget to slow down and smell the flowers. So slow down and enjoy the scenic wonders along the California coast. And now, here I am, at San Luis Obispo de Tolosa, the fifth mission on Fr. Serra's chain. The original missions were constructed with adobe walls and thatched roofs. At San Luis Obispo, hostile Indians using flaming arrows set the roofs afire, and finally, after three such fires, the roofs were replaced with red tiles, a first in the mission chain. Ruined by land reforms, as were most of the missions, this one survived as a parish church. The combination of belfry and vestibule is unique among the California missions. The original padre's residence is now the usual well-stocked museum.

Leaving the small town of San Luis Obispo by way of Rte. 101, I rode north through the pleasant village of Paso Robles. About ten miles north of Paso Robles, I accidentally spotted Mission San Miguel Arcángel, and while this mission was not founded by Fray Serra it definitely warrants a visit. All these missions instill a special sensation within one, maybe even a spiritual one. And now on to King City and, since the day was waning, I booked into a motel and had a nice dinner and a good night's sleep. With a trusty map and my untrusty sense of direction I followed roads without numbers till I found Mission San Antonio de Padua. This is the one mission that is a wee bit off the beaten path, which I felt really enhanced the beauty of its structures and the surrounding gardens. The old church and the entire quadrangle have been restored and rebuilt. In its beautiful but lonely location many miles from any town, this mission more than any other looks just as it did in early Spanish times. The elegant campaigner of burned brick stands unique among the bell walls of the mission chain. Behind the bell wall is a vault leading to the church itself. Since I had arrived at the mission early on the morning of June 13, I proceeded to do my thing with the Nikon.

I was interrupted by a friendly greeting extended by one Brother Joachim. During our casual talk, he mentioned how nice it was that my visit coincided with the feast day of St. Anthony, their patron saint. This reminded me that it was also my birthday, which was cause enough to have a celebration. So with Brother Joachim, a few padres, and their related visitors, I enjoyed a sumptuous breakfast. After the personal blessing by the padres I rode off, not into the sunset, but spiritually uplifted, over the mountainous road, not very far from the 5,882-foot mountain named Juniper Serra Peak, and on to oceanside Rte. 1.

Fifty-plus miles of cycling happiness led me to Monterey and Mission San Carlos Borromeo de Carmel, the second mission founded by Serra. It is situated more than 600 miles north of Mission San Diego. Why and how Fr. Serra traveled this distance or even why the missions were founded in the first place are other interesting stories. Look them up in the "Life of Father Serra" or in the big smart book. The Spanish expeditions into Mexico, with their religious, military, and political aspects, provide a wealth of intriguing perusal. This mission in Carmel was Fr. Serra's favorite and also his final resting place: He is buried neath the altar in this beautiful edifice. On its splendid site at the mouth of Carmel Valley, and overlooking the sea, this old mission has survived years of neglect but is now one of the outstanding historic landmarks of California. Much of the stateliness of its earlier days has been recaptured in the careful restorations of the building. The beauty of its gardens is unsurpassed, and the unique architecture of the church reflects the Moorish influence.

A glance at my road map indicated the scenic route that leads back to 101, El Camino Real. A perfectly enjoyable ride, spoiled only by my commuter-hour arrival at San Jose. Somehow, amidst all the confusion, I blundered onto Rte. 82, also named Camino Real, and Mission Santa Clara de Asís.

At one time this mission was the most prosperous of those in the north, although it suffered the same unfortunate destiny as other missions after the padres and Mexicans cast off the yolk of the Spanish royalty and later came under American rule. Santa Clara has been used as an educational institution since it was taken over by the Jesuits in 1851. Floods, earthquake, and fire successively destroyed three sets of mission buildings. The university chapel was built after the fire of 1926, its design a faithful reproduction of the old mission church of a century earlier. The campaigner contains the bells sent from Spain many years ago. This mission aroused the least amount of excitement within these weary bones of mine, possibly because I still ached from the hassles of the stop and go traffic en route.

After finding my way back to Rte. 101, I headed north for about fifty miles of no-fun traffic and located my final mission, Mission Dolores. When I realized I had ridden from Santa Clara to Mission Dolores without one wrong turn, I was shocked, since I definitely lack the instincts of a homing pigeon. In fact, many of the most interesting areas I have enjoyed in my travels have been the result of wrong turns.

The Mission San Francisco de Asís, founded in 1776, was named in honor of St. Francis, founder of the Franciscan Order. When the city took that name, the mission came to be known as Dolores, after the lake near the mission. This mission, the oldest building in the city of San Francisco, survived the great earthquake and fire of 1906. Its interior is much the same as the original. The decorated redwood ceiling beams created by Indian workmen remain. The wooden columns were painted to resemble Italian marble. Outside the church the old cemetery is as of yesteryear. The modern Mission Dolores Basilica was later built next to the mission.

Having completed my tour of the Serran Missions, and with time now on my side, I enjoyed the luxury of What to do? Now the Oakland Bay Bridge looked inviting and Sacramento revived romantic visions of the 1849 Gold Rush. So off I went and with a haphazard pattern found I-80, which, after ninety miles, led me into Sacramento and a night's sleep. California's capital city, the gold rush helped put Sacramento on the map. I followed Rte. 50 eastward to Placerville. On the way to Placerville, I shared a skimpy breakfast with a biker, older than either Tinker or me, a grisly old bugger who straddled an ancient Indian cycle that had surely seen better days. They looked like holdovers from the gold rush days. As we parted company, he made my day: "Drive safe, young fellow," says he.

Now the name Placerville intrigued me, so I checked out its two parts in the dictionary and found definitions. Since *ville* means "town," we are left with "Placer." The first line on "Placer" is "one who places things or objects," but the second definition is more pertinent. "Placer," according to the smart book, means "a deposit of gravel or sand containing gold particles large enough to be obtained by washing." More appropriately, definition number three says "any place where deposits are washed for valuable minerals." Thus, I arrived at my interpretation: "the town where deposits are washed, hopefully, for valuable minerals."

The "Gold Rush Trail" (Rte. 49), from Placerville south to the junction of Rte. 41 near Oakhurst, offers an interesting diversion from the monotonous interstates, so if you have the time, well, better to take it than not. Traveling south on Rte. 49, I soon hit Marshall Gold Discovery State Park. At most stops along the Gold Rush Trail, you will encounter exhibits or leftover relics of the '49 Gold Rush. I wonder if the Gold Rush of 1849 had anything to do with naming this trail Rte. 49. Riding south, Tinker carried me through aptly named towns, such as Dry Town, Sutter Creek, Angels Camp, Chinese Camp, each with a history all its own.

Sutter is, without doubt, the most pertinent name associated with the discovery of gold in California. John Sutter came to America from Switzerland and settled in California. At this time the Golden State was a province of Mexico. He gained title to 50,000 acres and soon became a prosperous rancher. As a result of the Mexican War, California attached to the US, and Sutter was all set, so it seemed. Then in 1848 an employee of Sutter, one James Marshall, discovered gold on Sutter's property. They became partners in a gold mining venture but, when the news leaked out, people of various occupations overran the property, seeking gold. Thus the start of the most famous gold rush of modern times. After a few years the rush faded and there were few new finds.

Traveling south down the Gold Rush Trail, I paused at many of the historical points of interest, and finally reached Oakhurst. At this point I continued on to Fresno, Bakersfield, Barstow and the ghost town of Calico, in that order. If route numbers turn you on, try these, from Placerville to Calico—49, 41, 99, 58, 15.

Calico was deserted after the gold rush days and is now an interesting, restored village replete with features designed to separate the tourists from their hard-earned cash. As I ambled about the village, I was accosted by two young Japanese lassies who had strayed from their tour group. They politely inquired if I was a "desert rat." Thinking they were joking, I replied, "That I am." I guess my dusty, frowzy appearance put the thought in their heads. Next scene, they had a stranger snap a few photos of the "desert rat" with one lassie on either side. I felt like a celebrity.

After my pleasant encounter with the Japanese tour group, Tinker led me eastward on Rte. 40. I set the cruise control on, well, let's just say the speed limit, and sat back and waited for lunch or Smokey Bear. Usually Smokey arrived first and after discovering an overage biker, it usually turned into a pleasant discussion about bikes, bikers, and my travels, and an admonition to slow down.

An uneventful and quite boring interstate trip, interrupted by a few motel stops, led me all the way to Johnson City, Tenn. Most motels in the middle third of our country, I found, were operated by immigrants from India, who seem to have an aversion to supplying towels. So register, go to your room, and then return to the office and request some towels.

My arrival in Johnson City was timing at its best, just in time for the opening party of the Motorcycling Doctors Association's annual meeting. After three days of educational seminars, business meetings, and parties, it was "on the road again."

Johnson City, a small town of about 14,000 population, is tucked away in the northeast corner of Tennessee. A short ride will get you to I-81 for a quick trip through Virginia to home. Traveling northeast diagonally through the Old Dominion State is a long ride, more than 300 miles, all in the same state. With my aversion to the interstates and not wishing to spend most of the day in one state, I chose to follow the Wilderness Road, originally called "Boone's Trace." This trail will lead you to Kentucky via the

Cumberland Gap, a gorge through the Cumberland Mountains near the junction of Kentucky, Tennessee, and Virginia. As I wandered north along winding, hilly roads, built to satisfy the most eager biker, I entered Daniel Boone National Forest. It seemed as if every few miles in this area the name Daniel Boone popped up. A very large portion of eastern Kentucky hosts the Boone National Forest, and even one of those infernal toll roads is called "Daniel Boone Parkway." Cincinnati (Ohio) International Airport is actually in Boone County, Kentucky. That name again. When I arrived home, with the name "Boone" still fresh in my mind, I latched onto a history book and read the life of this very interesting man. Well worth reading.

My totally enjoyable trek through Kentucky via secondary roads led me into West Virginia. I said good-bye to Kentucky as I passed through the hills, hills still home to the descendants of the first settlers, mostly Germans and Scots Irish. I expected to see the Hatfields and McCoys. Back on the interstate and other concrete slabs, I headed straight for New Jersey with just a few interruptions due to heavy showers.

And so, I arrived safely back home with a bountiful supply of pleasant memories of people, places, and happenings. Memories that will provide me with years of reminiscing, after these nomadic bones of mine are finally unable to straddle Tinker. These I will place in a "Book of Happy Memories" for future browsing.

VII.
Tunisian
Adventure

Along about January 1983, I was suffering the usual post-holiday blahs—like it was too cold and icy to bike, too cold to golf, and cabin fever was causing my feet to itch like hell. But in January where can you ease the itch? While poking through my usual pile of junk mail, I came across an invitation to join an Edelweiss bike tour to Tunisia. The encyclopedia told me Tunisia is located in Africa, and it also said Africa is warm. So . . . after much communicating back and forth, including many frantic phone calls, I was signed up and ready to relieve the itch.

Edelweiss Bike Tours is located in Austria and they offer guided tours to almost any place in the world. This agency will provide rental motorcycles, or you may ship your own bike to the starting point of your tour, in this case Austria, for a reasonable fee.

Since I owned a 1000cc BMW touring bike and had racked up more than 70,000 miles of cross-country travel on said bike, I was quite familiar with BMWs. I felt my bike was a little too heavy for desert travel so I opted for an 800cc BMW rental. This proved to be a wise choice—heavy enough for highway speeds and yet light enough for dirt, sand, gravel, or whatever. Many times it was "whatever."

My itinerary called for a flight to Zurich, Switzerland, followed by a connecting flight to Innsbruck, Austria, where I was to be met by a tour rep and a ride to nearby Ubermeiming. While anxiously awaiting my departure date, I got to thinking, "This is an awful long way to travel just to get warm by wiggling my toes in the sands of the Sahara." So I changed my plans to include an extension to Vienna, via train, for three days of sightseeing.

The overnight flight to Zurich was, except for a brief glimpse of the Matterhorn, tiring and boring, as most overseas flights are. The hop from Zurich to Innsbruck, on the other hand, held my interest for the entire short flight. The smaller plane, flying at a lower altitude permitted excellent views of the snow-covered Alps. At Innsbruck Airport, I got a taxi to the railroad station and boarded the next available train for Vienna. The train ride to Vienna was about the nicest trip via rail I have ever experienced. The fast, clean train, railing through the beautiful countryside, the efficient meal service, and the on-time arrival made it a memorable journey. A taxi delivered me to an old, exquisite downtown hotel which was my base for the next three days.

Each morning, I shared a bus tour with a mixed bag of tourists, none of whom spoke a familiar tongue. As usual, the tour guide was well versed in the history, culture, and other aspects of his subject, in this case, Vienna. Still, as the guide droned on and on, I snoozed on and on. Occasionally a bump in the road awakened me to catch a bit of history that I had already snoozed through in high school.

At each stop we were herded through some important palace, museum, opera house, or government building. I managed to stay awake long enough to learn a few facts and anecdotes regarding Vienna, the capital of Austria. It is located along the famous Danube River, and was once one of the most important political and cultural centers of the world. It was the seat of the

Holy Roman Empire for 300 hundred years. I must admit I was impressed with our visit to the Imperial (Hofburg) Palace, Schönbrunn Palace, museums, et cetera. For many years Vienna was the music capital of the world and is credited with giving birth to the waltz during the seventeenth century.

Most of the bus tours left me time for my own afternoon walking tours. Armed with a map and my decrepit sense of direction[11], I managed to stumble on some very interesting aspects of this fine city. Vienna was once a walled city, a wall that has since been replaced by a grand boulevard, appropriately called the Ringstrasse. The "ring," or circle street, ensured against getting lost, or seemed to. I wandered through many areas and neighborhoods, rode the trolley cars, checked out the subway station, and visited St. Stephen's Cathedral, Vienna's most famous landmark. It was begun in the year 1147.

As the afternoon wore on, I realized that in spite of the confining Ringstrasse, my sense of direction was, in fact, entirely defunct. I was lost. Like a good tourist in trouble I hailed a taxi. When I mentioned my hotel, the cabby, with heavy, guttural, but excellent English directed me: "One block north, turn left, and you're there. It's too short for a cab ride." I climbed aboard anyway and told him to take the long way and fill me in on what I missed during my walking tour. European taxi drivers, unlike their New York counterparts, are professionals in every sense of the word and are well informed in history and other mind stimulating bits of knowledge. In '83, at least, they made wonderful tour guides at reasonable rates. From this engaging cabby, I learned that in 1683 Polish King John III Sobieski led the combined forces of Europe against the Ottoman Turks and defeated them, in a battle just north of Vienna. He also informed me that the Jews were made to scrub the streets of Vienna during Hitler's regime—just a few items of many that this well-informed

11 To be politically correct, I do not have a decrepit sense of direction. I am "directionally challenged."

cabby imparted to me before we said our good-bye at my hotel. This man could have qualified as a history instructor.

After a too-sound sleep, I missed my wake-up call, and thus I also missed my return train to Innsbruck. In a mad dash, with the help of the front desk, I did make a reservation for a flight, and phoned my tour rep to skip the train arrival and meet me at the airport instead. All went well and I did arrive at our base, Gasthof Schwarz Hotel, *sans* my toilet articles, which I hope some hotel worker found useful. My arrival was just in time for our get-acquainted dinner. At this dinner, I was introduced to the sixteen other pairs of itching feet, and received the first of our daily briefings. A very busy day was completed with a short trial ride around the village of Ubermeiming to familiarize myself with this strange rental bike, an R80 BMW.

Six a.m. the next morning, I climbed aboard the BMW and headed with the group for Genoa, Italy, via the Brenner Pass through the Italian Alps. At 4,500 feet it is the lowest pass through the Alps. Snow aplenty, but clear roads. Approximately four hundred miles of good road lay before us. This we knew beforehand, but the heavy rain for much of the autostrada route was unexpected, uncomfortable, and unwarm. For this part of the trip we divided into two groups, fast and slow. My roommate, a minister from Minnesota, and I opted for the slow group, figuring we could better get the feel of European riding. Well, "slow" meant 80 to 90 mph (approximately 130 kph). I hasten to mention that speed does not necessarily mean recklessness. All the riders were well qualified, mentally, physically, in equipment, and in experience. Apparently, there was no speed limit on the Italian highways, at least at this time.

South of the pass, we followed Italy's version of a superhighway and of course our first stop was a tollbooth. I didn't have any liras, only krones, so the toll collector proceeded to give me a hard time. But when he discovered I was American and not Austrian, suddenly, all was well. The opposite of Nicaragua.

As we headed south, our schedule forced us to bypass Milan, and thus, we missed a visit to this city of one million residents, a city that was 60% destroyed during WWII. Milan is also renowned for its great Gothic cathedral and that other great edifice, the church where St. Ambrose baptized St. Augustine. And of course, let us not neglect to mention the convent of Santa Maria delle Grazie where Da Vinci's "Last Supper" is painted on the refectory wall.

We all arrived at the ferry in Genoa on time. Genoa is another city of about one million and is the birthplace of Christopher Columbus. It is Italy's largest port in passenger and freight traffic. After endless paperwork we boarded the *Habib*, our home for the next twenty-four hours. Of course, the intricate details were efficiently handled by our yodeling tour director, Werner Wachter. As the *Habib* sailed out of this busy port, we looked back at the eye-pleasing backdrop of the surrounding Ligurian Apennine Mountains.

A fun day to relax on deck or visit the bar and get acquainted with our American, Canadian, German, Austrian, and Swiss comrades. After a few cool beers, language was no barrier. We also learned that our Tunisian vessel hadn't yet discovered the wonders of such amenities as toilet tissue. Arrival in Tunisia meant more paperwork and ID checks. Finally we were allowed to debark and regroup.

We headed through the boulevards and the narrow, crowded streets of Tunis, the capital city of Tunisia, to the Tunis Hilton, a luxury hotel (the last one for us on this trek). A brief word of advice: Whenever you travel in strange lands always top off your fuel tank at each opportunity and carry your own supply of sanitary needs.

Our route from Tunis took us to Carthage, where we viewed some Roman ruins. I was surprised to learn that there are eight major sites containing varying amounts of well-preserved Roman ruins, many of which we viewed as we circled the country. Also located in Carthage is one of six neatly kept Allied war cemeteries where about 3,000 American soldiers are interred, casualties of the World War II Tunisian battles. From Carthage, our trail led us westward, through the northern hills, on winding, narrow blacktop and, sometimes, gravel or just plain dirt roads. Small villages with plenty of friendly, smiling faces. Periodic roadblocks staffed with friendly and courteous police, always well dressed. Sometimes there would be a military checkpoint to see our credentials, but the treatment was always friendly and polite.

After a beautiful, exciting ride we found ourselves in Tabarka. Tabarka ("bushy place") is a small town sitting along the bright sands of the Mediterranean with the beautiful mountains of Khroumiri in the background. A murky causeway leads you out to the base of a large promontory. A trail, sometimes grass, sometimes dirt, will take you up, or nearly up, to Genoese Fort perched atop the promontory. Of course, my roommate and I followed the trail to the point where we could go no farther. After a few photos of the spectacular view, we had to manually reverse the direction of our bikes because the very narrow trail prevented any U-turns. Tabarka is noted as a center for the collection and shipping of cork from the trees of the Khroumiri Mountains, not to forget an ancient history of marble, timber, and mineral exploitation.

Our overnight stay in Tobarka ended with an early breakfast and our daily briefing, then on toward Djebel Chambi, at slightly more than 5,000 feet, Tunisia's highest mountain. Throughout Tunisia we traveled in pairs or small groups. Usually I rode with my roommate, the Reverend McCall. Often a husband-wife team from Canada joined us. Nightfall found us camping on the semiarid desert near Kasserine, the WWII battle area. I soon learned the desert is as cold at night, as it is hot, during the day. Coming together each evening for chow and again in the morning for breakfast and the day's briefing, I learned what a fine effort our tour director made assigning roommates for such a varied group. Consider the fact that he had five nationalities, four languages, and also a range of ages from about 30 to 60 plus (need I mention who was 60 plus?), two married couples, and two pretty, single young ladies—a varied group for only twenty individuals, but as we left the ferry in Tunis, we were already more like one big family.

After a very cold night in sleeping bags, the day's briefing, and the usual breakfast of oranges, bread, dates, cheese, bread, wine, and more bread, we departed Kasserine and headed south to Nefta. En route we drifted off to visit a few isolated oases. Very easy to lose the way even though we all had maps and our daily route was outlined for us. Getting lost became routine for most of the troupe, but we always arrived at our destination pretty much on schedule. Nefta is a beautiful oasis in the Eastern Erg of the Sahara. It was necessary to dig wells to the depth of 2,100 feet to support the 200,000 palms in this oasis.

Day by day the tour grew in interest and beauty, and after leaving Nefta we all agreed: Nefta could not be surpassed. But it was. From Nefta to Douz is about one hundred miles across the Chott Djerid (salt lake or flats). Actually, the chott stretches from the Gulf of Gabes, 200 miles west into Algeria. Some parts are below sea level and in the winter months, as the water table rises, it becomes an impassable quagmire. When the water recedes, the salt remains and a sort of causeway is then bulldozed across the flats. At times you must ride through shallow water. So schedule your own visit during or after April. With more than 500,000 palm trees (primarily dates), Douz is the ultimate oasis. The palm trees live about fifty years and provide dates for food, palm wine for drink, stones to crush into fodder or ersatz coffee, fiber to weave into rope, and also fronds to make thatch and furniture, not to mention trunks to build roofs and footbridges. From Tunis southward, we encountered dogs, cats, goats, sheep, donkeys, and now we can add the noisy, nasty camel. Since it was camel market day, the place abounded with the smelly creatures. Good hotels were few and far between, but in Douz we had a lovely one; it even had a swimming pool and entertainment.

The next leg of our trek took us from Douz to Matmata, from comparative luxury to squalor, and all within 150 miles. As you probably surmised, each day's ride wasn't too great mile-wise, but the road or lack of it dictated how far is far. Somewhere between Douz and Matmata, we lost the trail and wandered into a small colony. My cleric roommate, having lived his early years in Lebanon, was familiar with Arabic and thus able to get us back on track with the help of the natives. The five-mile error proved interesting. We always felt secure along the road, since a light pickup trailed us. It carried our excess baggage (bedrolls and so forth) and spare parts. The only problem was that many times we lost the sand-covered road.

The Matmata area is inhabited by the pit-dwelling Berbers, the aboriginal people of North Africa, often called the Amazaght people. Again we were impressed by the simple way of life and the friendliness of these most interesting people. At one point a family invited us to see their cave dwelling, a large pit with rooms dug into the sides. Even a room for the sheep and goats.

As we headed toward our evening rendezvous, I marveled at the scenery and the Berbers' mode of life, little did I know that our sleep for that night was to be in a pit. These pits are up to 30 feet deep and the rooms are dug into the sides. They offered great protection from the heat with a constant cool temperature. A few candles provided light and heat. As usual no luxuries such as toilet tissue, but after twenty-four hours aboard the *Habib*, I had made sure I didn't leave the Tunis Hilton unequipped. As an extra treat, we were entertained by a Berber drum band.

Anyone who roams North Africa, at some point will experience "couscous," and after doing so will wonder, "What was that?" Well couscous is to North Africa, what poi is to Hawaii, and now you know as much as I do. It seems that couscous is served on any or all occasions or excuses.

After questioning numerous natives and fellow visitors, I learned couscous is couscous. When I returned home to the land of oatmeal, grits, and martinis one of my first acts was to dig out the encyclopedia. The big book says that couscous is a dish traditionally eaten with lamb. In the absence of lamb, anything will do. It is made of flour, plus the "anything," granulated and cooked by steaming over the vapors of broth or meat. Semolina comes into the act someplace here but that is a too detailed story for this essay. Poi on the other hand is a native Hawaiian food made from the taro root. It is first cooked, ground to a paste, and then fermented. And now, being forewarned, feel free to avoid both dishes.

After Matmata we headed north toward the resort island of Djerba and a nice clean hotel on the Mediterranean Sea, good swimming, and few people. The isle of Djerba is a small flat island with a few excellent hotels and a lovely beach. While patiently waiting for the ferry to float us to Djerba, I noticed two youngsters watching the proceedings. Suddenly one lad politely dropped his pants, did his business, and then replaced his drawers, an example of the lack of sanitary conditions. Natives of the isle grow olives and palms, weave carpets, and fish.

Here on the island of Djerba, we had a day of leisure, visiting Houmt-Souk ("market quarter," the largest market and town on the island) and enjoying our own competitions, slow races, and so on. We welcomed a day of rest before our run to Mahares for another scratchy camp-out. Dawn arrived, as did our usual breakfast of cheese, bread, tomatoes, bread, dates, wine, oranges, and don't forget the bread. With approval from our director, my riding buddy and I opted to skip Mahares, a so-so fishing village on the shores of the Gulf of Gabes, and continue north through the quiet modern city of Sfax. A hurried visit and on to El Djem to view the leftover Roman coliseum there—definitely worthy of a photo shoot. I think the Romans must have been in an architectural rut, it seems that all over the then known world they left duplicates of what's in Rome: baths, amphitheaters, the forum with its temples, and the coliseum.

And now we are back on the narrow macadam to the resort city of Sousse. As you may surmise, we are not far from the Mediterranean coast as we head north, leaving the Sahara behind. In Sousse we booked into a nice hotel and, after a much needed shower, gave ourselves a walking tour of this interesting city. The beautiful beach had to compete with a wide variety of attractions: the medina, museum, cinemas, sidewalk cafes, and card-playing natives, many with hashish pipes close at hand. Sousse, and practically every other city in Tunisia, has a history dating back to the days of the Phoenicians, Hannibal and his elephants, the Punic Wars, the Roman Empire, the Byzantine Empire, Vandal and Arab invasions, and let's not forget World Wars I and II. Speaking of the numerous wars, it was in the year 1985 that Rome and Carthage, now a suburb of Tunis, signed a pact to formally end the ancient Punic Wars. History tells us that more than two thousand years ago, the Romans overpowered the Carthaginians, razed their ancient capital, plowed its ruins into the earth, and sowed the soil with salt so nothing could grow again. Approximately two millennia is a long time to wait for a truce. But alas, it was now time to hit the sack and get ready for an early exit from Sousse.

Early morning found us backtracking in a westerly direction so as to catch up to our group. We planned to meet in Kairouan, and we did. The ancient city of Kairouan lies on an important caravan route, thus the name, which means "caravan." It is walled and the streets too narrow for any modern vehicles. This tends to preserve the true personality of this, the fourth holiest city of the Islamic faith. Tradition dictates that four trips to Kairouan equals one trip to Mecca. The 69,000 people of Kairouan make carpets, leather, and brassware, and grow most of Tunisia's apricots. An unusual sidelight here was a view of the blindfolded camels harnessed to wooden yokes and walking in a continuous circle, drawing water from the well. Of course, outside the walls of ancient Kairouan a more modern city has developed. Leaving this unique city I felt I was already leaving Tunisia, knowing that our next stop would be our final one in this country.

So after a not too exciting ride, here we were, back in the modern (or almost modern) city of Tunis, where more than one million of the six million inhabitants of Tunisia live. Our overnight stay at the Hilton brought out the fact that our adventure, our camaraderie, you might even say our affair, was about to end. So amid many drinks and quickly arranged parties we said our formal good-byes.

Next day while waiting to board the infamous *Habib*, I observed a wide variety of people and vehicles returning from their desert treks. Land rovers bedecked with goatskin water bags and treads to aid navigation over loose or deep sand, small trucks, and plenty of motorcycles. Once on board we now had twenty-four hours to unwind, but instead, we partied and repeated our farewells. At this point, we were a very close group and didn't need much excuse to party. We also learned how easy it was to crash the first class lounge and movies. The soft life as opposed to the crowded, smelly steerage class we were assigned to. Originally we were scheduled to board a Danish ship for the inbound and outbound voyages but the line's franchise was canceled, so we wound up on the Tunisian German-built *Habib*.

Unlike the southward journey, the trip from Genoa back to Innsbruck, that quaint little town nestled in the valley of the River Inn, was pleasant all the way—beautiful sunshine, and clear roads, if a wee bit chilly. Back at our base hotel, Gasthof Schwarz, we had our final dinner and party. Early next morning the tour director and my minister roommate personally delivered me to the airport (one last farewell!), and on to Zurich and then New York

The welcome home by my sons, their wives, and my grandchildren made me very happy, but I must admit I reserve a warm spot in my heart for the beautiful people on the Tunisian adventure. I guess bikers, the world over, are the greatest people.

Since returning to home, I have been asked, on more than a few occasions, "What or who is Tunisia?" Well, Tunisia is the most northern country in Africa. It's about the size of England and is wedged between Libya and Algeria, with a good amount of Mediterranean coastline. In the north, the well-watered mountains and valleys make for a wide variety of fruits and vegetables. In the south, more than 10,000 square miles of the Sahara Desert are dotted with the always interesting oases. In between, you find the semiarid areas and the *chotts*, the salt flats mentioned earlier. While the main language is Arabic, a knowledge of French is helpful. To a lesser degree, Italian is spoken.

The six-million-plus inhabitants are a young group overall, 55% under the age of 20 years. The aborigines are the nomadic Berbers, but down through the years of invasions, many strains were assimilated so that now you will see light skins and blue eyes, and all the shades to the deepest black. While the shades of skin vary, their smiling faces and friendliness are constant, despite their minimal worldly or material possessions.

The monetary unit is the dinar, which in turn breaks down into millemes (thousandths). Thus, one thousand millemes equal one dinar. The dinar is noteworthy in that the government prohibits the import or export of their currency. This means Tunisia fixes the rate of exchange and thus is not bothered by foreign markets. It also means that you should carry only enough dinars to serve your immediate needs. You can't take them home.

Since getting rid of French control in 1959, President Bourguiba has done a great job in all facets of government. While the number of cities is comparatively small, you will have no trouble finding a variety of interesting items to buy. Rugs and carpets are attractive to those on a relatively limited budget. I haggled for four sheepskins, a hashish pipe, and a couple of brass plates with misspelled inscriptions. These brass plates are hammered out, before your eyes, by local artists, but with no knowledge of Arabic, who's to check the schoolwork? Incidentally, my souvenir hashish pipe was never questioned by Tunisian, Austrian, Swiss, or American customs. (Not that I intended to ever use it.)

Tunisia, the land of Islam, preserves a profound respect for places of worship. Muslims meet at the mosque five times each day, at the hour of prayer. You must be properly dressed and respectful of the customs and observances of the religious. While Islam is the most widespread faith, there are places of worship other than Muslim. In Tunis, you will find Roman Catholic, Anglican, Protestant, and Russian and Greek Orthodox churches, and a Jewish synagogue. A valid passport is all that was necessary for U.S. citizens to enter Tunisia in 1983. Liquor and tobacco were permitted, in specified amounts, but foreign currency was permitted with no limit. On the "no-no" list: Tunisian dinars, weapons, drugs, explosives, and obscene publications. Once again I recommend you do your homework regarding the culture, religion, politics, and customs before your visit to any foreign soil.

In Tunisia you are also permitted to carry two cameras and twenty rolls of film, and any electrical needs such as shavers and hair driers. Electric current is 110 volts, although some modern hotels may offer 220 volts. You may leave Tunisia with all articles purchased that correspond with the amount of money exchanged.

Another question asked by a few of my biker friends is "How do European bikers compare to American bikers?" Generally speaking both have many fine qualities, such as friendliness, a carefree attitude, a love of biking and probably the most common trait, the spirit of camaraderie and the ever present willingness to help a fellow biker.

The driving ability is about equal. If the Europeans have an advantage, it is that they do more fast riding because of fewer restrictions and less traffic. The one area where I feel they outshine us is in their approach to biking. I felt that most tend to be better dressed, not fashion-wise, but with safety in mind, that is, helmets, full leathers, gloves, boots, and well-tuned machines. Fairings and windshields were not too common, which in turn leads to more full-face helmets. Tank bags appear to be more popular than our American saddlebags. They also camped out more regularly. I feel that what differences there are, exist because of conditions such as the economy, availability of motels, traffic and traffic laws, weather, and any number of minor factors.

While Arabic may appear difficult or impossible to most people, a few definitions may help:

chott	salt lake
medina	an Arab city or part of one, often walled
minaret	tall, slender tower attached to a Muslim mosque and surrounded by one or more balconies from which a muezzin calls the faithful to prayer
muezzin	in Islam, a crier who calls the faithful to prayer five times per day
marabout	a Muslim holy man or hermit of North Africa, revered by Berbers
sebkha	salt flat
souk	market or marketplace
sirocco	a hot, dry, dusty southerly wind

Please remember these thoughts and observations are based on a wonderful excursion in the year 1983.

VIII.
Favorite
Roads

After looking back on my cross-country rides, I can't help but feel deeply grateful and thankful. Grateful to my family for tolerating my dedicated wanderlust. Thankful to God for the gift of good health, the gift that enabled me to enjoy wandering about this land of ours and others. And while counting my blessings, let me not forget this great country that He has given us.

How lucky we are in the United States. Endless travel opportunities, whether you like the mountains, the forests, lakes, shore, desert, or plains, even volcanoes—they're all there awaiting your visit. Our national parks offer a wide variety of scenic wonders, from the depths of Death Valley to the tip of Mt. McKinley, unbelievable beauty. Beauty that man could never match, even in his dreams.

Of course, my feelings lead me to urge you to enjoy these wonders from atop a motorcycle. Why? So as to better appreciate the world about you using all your senses, that is, feeling the fresh air on your face, and occasionally a few drops of heavy dew. You feel the rhythm of the road, the ups and downs, and those delightful bends in the byways—all contribute to the exhilaration of biking. Also, you hear the sounds of the world first hand, like the melodic tweeting of the birds, the chirping crickets as you camp at nightfall, and sometimes the sound of Smokey Bear's siren as he approaches for a brief chat. And then there are the smells of the woodlands, the flowers, the diesels, and of course the wood-burning stoves that signal the arrival of fall, especially in the Northeast. Last, but not least, use your sense of sight to enjoy the marvels laid out before you. Lest you become hypnotized by the wonders of our countryside, pull off the road and enjoy to your heart's content. Whether it be a rest stop, scenic overlook, or evening stopover, you are sure to meet the nicest people in the world, fellow travelers.

Now if you think you've seen all of America's beauty, just jump across our northern border and enjoy the Niagara Falls from the Canadian side. Travel the Maritime Provinces and then head west on the Trans-Canada Highway over the seemingly endless plains, until the eastern slopes of the Rockies appear in the distance. Keep riding and eventually, you will reach Jasper National Park, view the glaciers, then Lake Louise and the surrounding scenic areas. Still have time? Go north into the Yukon Territory and, after sampling the Klondike, you will be tempted to keep going farther. Well go for it. Now you might as well continue back into the United States—Alaska. If Alaska doesn't stir the gypsy in your soul, just go home and retire to the rocking chair.

If you feel our northern neighbor is too cool, then why not try our southern exposure—Mexico and places farther south? Here you will experience a few different delights, such as dormant volcanoes, rugged mountains, ancient cultural remains of the Toltecs, Aztecs, and the Maya, and don't forget the living Indian cultures such as the Zapotec, the many Mayan communities, and those admirable Cuna Indians, who thrive on the San Blas Islands off the Caribbean coast of Panama. A study of these cultures could fill a lifetime of interesting study.

After returning home from each journey, naturally, you will spend some time reliving your experiences. And, of course, certain roads leave a deeper impression than others. As I reflect on my travels, the one trail that stands out most prominently is the "Going to the Sun Road," located in northern Montana. While I had heard of Glacier National Park, I was not aware of "Going to the Sun Road," which traverses the park. I discovered it in a roundabout way.

After departing my home base in New Jersey and four wonderful days on the road, I arrived in Ouray, Colorado, for the Motorcycling Doctors Association annual meeting. Three days of happy reunions, educational lectures, and rides through the scenic San Juan Mountains passed all too quickly. Foregoing the usual late morning good-byes, I headed out very early, hoping to reach Vancouver, British Columbia, in time for the Serra International Convention one day hence and approximately 1,400 miles distant. Fourteen hundred miles of completely unfamiliar roads—it didn't take me long to realize that this was one more silly dream. (Silly and unfeasible dreams are also among my few perfections.)

Leaving Ouray, I headed north to Grand Junction, Co., and then west into the Beehive State, Utah. I then continued in a northwest slant through Idaho into Oregon. After about nine hundred miles of pleasant cruising with few or no traffic problems, I began to tire. Foolishly, I continued on in the darkness of night when suddenly something was amiss. I had fallen asleep, probably for just a second, and I drifted off the road, but my Guardian Angel steered me down a dirt construction road. Now fully awake and frightened, I found myself amidst the construction equipment. My watch indicated two a.m., so I climbed aboard a backhoe's uncomfortable, but very welcome seat, and slept for two hours. I sheepishly relate this very stupid and dangerous experience with the hope that I can prevent others from doing likewise. When you feel tired, take a break.

As dawn broke, I followed the scenic route along the river that separates the states of Washington and Oregon, the Columbia. At various points you are offered a view of Mount Hood in the distance. Mt. Hood is an 11,000-foot peak located in the Cascade Range, east of Portland, Oregon. About mid-morning, having learned my "don't drive when sleepy" lesson, I caught a few hours of shut-eye on a very uncomfortable picnic bench, at a roadside park. Circling Portland, I picked up I-5 North, which led me to Seattle. The Seattle area brought me back to reality— beaucoup traffic, amply supplied with wild drivers. Most of us tend to think our own area has a monopoly on careless drivers, but as you travel any metropolitan area you will see that careless driving is a national problem.

Finally, twenty-nine hours after leaving Ouray I arrived in Vancouver, the largest city in the Canadian province of British Columbia. This city of approximately one-half million population enjoys the benefits of numerous parks, and rail, road, and air connections to all Canadian cities and many in the US. After registering at the Hyatt Regency for the Serra International Convention and stashing my limited luggage in my fancy quarters, I returned, and as directed by the attendant, I parked Tinker in a safe area, which also included bicycles. The accommodations, service, meals, and programs were A-One, and I wish I could say the same for the attitude of some Canadians toward us Yankees. To give one example, apparently the bicyclists didn't like the idea of sharing with motorcycles, so they left a mean and most inhospitable note attached to Tinker, including nasty comments regarding Americans, which I ignored. On getaway day I loaded and cranked up Tinker, but it was a no-go. A brief check revealed a spark plug wire had been removed by the gracious Canadian cyclists. After replacing said wire, Tinker was ready to roll, but not before I left a gentle reminder that two can play the game. I truly hope they enjoyed my answer to their prank.

Anyway, now I was on my way and once out of the Vancouver area, away from the local traffic, I connected to Canadian Rte. 3. Riding this very scenic trail, which was not designed for those in a hurry, I did enjoy the continuing changes, first heading north, then south, while yet maintaining its eastward trend. After an all-day ride of approximately five hundred miles, I departed Canada near the town of Creston. Dropping down into Idaho, I enjoyed some more scenic pleasures as I glided over US Rte. 2 into Kalispell, Montana.

A good night's sleep prepared me well for the thrills that were yet to come. As I drifted off to dreamland, the name Jimmie Davis came to mind. Who? Jimmie Davis, one of my favorite country singers from my post-high school days, is a member of the Country Music Hall of Fame, twice governor of Louisiana, recording artist, songster (he sang "You Are My Sunshine" and claimed to have written it), movie star, author, businessman, schoolteacher, and lecturer. He offered no advice, just caution: "If you don't know where you are going, you'd better not start." I always knew where I was going but I not necessarily how I would get there. I guess that's what makes getting there so exciting.

From Kalispell, I headed northeast to Lake McDonald and the western entry to Going to the Sun Road. Whether you traverse this scenic trail east to west or vice versa, matters not. The beauty, thrills, excitement are the same. From Lake MacDonald, I wound my way upward in a northeasterly direction, interrupted by numerous stops to photograph some of the forest-rimmed lakes and a few of the fifty glaciers. Tunnels are cut through the overhanging cliffs, and a few of these tunnels offer cutouts to permit a more accessible view of the wondrous sights. Eventually the road reaches its peak as it passes over the Continental Divide at 6,600-foot-high Logan Pass. The eastern downward, winding slopes of the divide equal the thrills of the western slopes. The rocky walls along the way still exhibited a coating of snow or ice, even though it was early summer. Finally, St. Mary Lake appeared, the reluctant end to a joyous ride that left me hypnotized by the splendor laid out before me. This highway and the surrounding Glacier National Park are not only for bikers. It offers numerous trails and campsites for nature lovers of all degrees. No shortage of lakes either, more than two hundred of them, fed by the fifty glaciers—they fulfill the wildest dream of any camper or hiker. And the variety of wildlife, large and small, complete this fantastic picture. I got a glimpse of a grizzly from a safe distance. Make that a *very* safe distance. Incidentally, this road is closed in the winter. Enough said. If you are ever in the Glacier National Park area, be sure you experience my nomination for the most scenic road in the United States, Going to the Sun Road. I was tempted to repeat the journey east to west, but tempus fugit, and my schedule demanded the most direct route to Great Falls, Montana (although not before I entered this road in my book of memories).

Great Falls meant a most pleasant visit with my St. Louis U buddy and family. A bountiful cookout offered the opportunity to overeat, etc. The "etc." means soft drinks and brew and the other stuff. Before departing, I was treated to a round of golf with borrowed clubs, just to prove to my friend that I had not lost any of my golfing errors.

Many roads have often been given the title of "Most Scenic Road in the US," and rightfully so. My personal choices are, as you might suspect, biased. They're generally influenced by my love of cycling, and my love of mountains, woodlands, and deserts.

After the Going to the Sun Road, the Blue Ridge Parkway merits the highest spot on my list of favorite roads. Many years ago my wife and I, along with our four children, rode the Blue Ridge Parkway in a comfortable station wagon. We enjoyed a leisurely trip from south to north, taking many stops to allow the kids to run off their bottled-up energy. The many streams and small animals were the perfect solution. As much as I enjoyed this family trip, I feel you must do it by motorcycle to fully appreciate all that this trail has to offer. But, alas, I wander, so back to the beginning of my second ride up the Blue Ridge Parkway.

One day after visiting friends in Kentucky, with plenty of time to spare, I said my good-byes and headed south for an overnight stay near Maryville, Tennessee. Next morning found me riding south to Fontana Lake. A brief visit to Fontana Dam, in North Carolina, was well worth the expended time. The dam is the highest (480 feet) of the fifty-one dams controlled by the TVA (Tennessee Valley Authority) and was finished in 1940. As expected, if you dam a river, you are going to have a lake, and maybe more. This in turn resulted in many recreational facilities and a very positive effect on the area's economy. The TVA is credited with the taming of the Tennessee River and introducing electricity to much of a seven-state area. This area was populated by impoverished inhabitants and had little industry. Thus, the TVA converted a depressed area into a recreational and industrial success while becoming the nation's largest utility firm of that time.

A short, eye-pleasing jaunt from Fontana Dam led me to a small town in Cherokee County, North Carolina, and I think the town was also called Cherokee. This area is part of a Cherokee reservation. Cherokee has, as would be expected, a high percentage of Cherokee residents, an energetic and inventive group, in this case dedicated to helping the tourist spend a few bucks. I was happy to part with a few shekels just to play the game. My favorite attraction starred a tightrope-walking chicken. This attraction, like the others, was designed to keep the inhabitants' Cadillacs filled with high-test petrol. After my enjoyable encounter with the chickens, I rode to Asheville, North Carolina—kind of a resort town, offering the usual selection of motels, service stations, fast food outlets, etc. It is a city of approximately 60,000 people in the Blue Ridge Mountains. These mountains stretch from Pennsylvania to Georgia and are a part of the Appalachian

Mountains. The mountains range from five to sixty miles wide, with individual peaks of 2,000 to 6,000 feet. Near Asheville, I connected to the Blue Ridge Parkway. This wandering, twisting ribbon extends approximately 500 miles from the northern Georgia border to Skyline Drive near Waynesboro, Va. Actually, this parkway (the BRP) connects the Great Smoky Mountains with Shenandoah National Park. An early start up the Blue Ridge Parkway had me enthralled with the twisting, up-and-down concrete.

When you ride this beautiful trail, allow yourself plenty of time to pull off and savor the plentiful sights laid out before you. The countryside offers an abundant supply of wildflowers, a variety of trees and smaller plants (seven hundred), fungi, a wide assortment of birds and small animals, and many rustling streams. And you can add three rivers that flow through the mountains, the Roanoke, Potomac, and James. When you read about trees, have you ever noticed that oaks are always sturdy, elms shady, pines shivering, and aspens quaking?

At various points, you may choose to exit the BRP and visit any of many towns for an overnight stay. I-81 is never too far away. I would suggest that you make this ride a leisurely one, and plan to lay over one or two nights so that you can enjoy the complete beauty of the area. If you are in a hurry, take monotonous Interstate 81 and fly home.

I took so many breaks to soak up the off-road sights that after traveling about halfway up the parkway, I was forced to leave it and seek a place for an evening of rest. I happened on a town near Natural Bridge, located between Roanoke and Lexington. Here I enjoyed the usual shower, dinner, and a very sound sleep. Next morning, before leaving the area, I paid a brief visit to Natural Bridge. It didn't compare to the Grand Canyon but was interesting enough to make me look it up in the big book later. Like so many areas in Virginia, Natural Bridge played a part in the Revolutionary War. The big book says that Natural Bridge was used as a shot tower in that war. Shot tower?[12]

Back on the BRP, I cycled north, thinking this trail must have been designed with bikers in mind. Near Waynesboro, Va., I connected to Skyline Drive, which is a continuation of the Blue Ridge Parkway, and rode through the Shenandoah National Park. More scenic wonders and more roads designed for motorcyclists. A short distance off Skyline Drive sits the Luray Caverns, which make for an interesting layover. When I neared Winchester, Va., I rode northeast to Harpers Ferry, which is located in the Blue Ridge Mountains at the junction of the Shenandoah and Potomac Rivers. It is where West Virginia, Virginia, and Maryland meet. Maybe you recall from your high school history class that Harpers Ferry is famous (or notorious, depending on your viewpoint) as the site of John Brown's ill-fated raid on a U.S. armory. One of the events leading up to the outbreak of the American Civil War.

I did a walk-through of the area but, since the restoration project was not quite complete, I didn't dally too long. Harpers Ferry is definitely worth a visit, especially for you history buffs.

I keep telling myself "I have plenty of time," and suddenly I realize I'm out it, so it's back to the office, pronto. When short of time, head for the nearest interstate going your way. In my case I-81 fit the need. I-81 led me to Rte. 78 and ultimately New Jersey, approximately 250 miles distant, just in time to resume my work schedule and plan for my next excursion. This past jaunt cured my wanderlust for, well, a while. But without work I cannot wander, so it's back to work, reliving my recent tour and dreaming of the next one.

---

12 Lead shot used for guns was produced by dropping hot liquid lead from high structures called shot towers. The globs solidified by the time they landed in ground-level water basins, where they also finished cooling.

As I stated previously, my selection of favorite roads is based on the scenery: lakes, glaciers, mountains, trees, deserts, animals, and the characteristics of the road as they relate to cycling. The curves, the ups and downs, all add to the excitement of the trip, be it short or extended. While the "Going to the Sun" road and the Blue Ridge Parkway left the deepest impression on me, there are many more roads that may not make the top ten, but they do stir the mind—trails such as the Natchez Trace, Oregon Trail, Donner Pass, Rte. 49 Gold Rush Trail, and that route along the Hudson River, the old Storm King Highway. Let's not forget Highway 12 in southern Utah, although I only rode it at times and in selected areas, usually as I headed for my favorite, Bryce Canyon. Highway 12 has been touted among the top ten scenic highways in America by Car and Driver magazine. This trail wanders 120 miles through canyons, red-rock cliffs, forests, and mountains as it traverses three national parks and three state parks.

On many occasions I have attempted to follow the aforementioned historic trails, but modern highway changes have made it difficult if not impossible to retrace the pathways of our early American explorers. Historic highway markers help somewhat, if you can find them. I have never heard any of the interstate highways selected for the top-ten list, but I would have to give an honorable mention to a short portion of I-90 that runs from Sioux Falls, South Dakota, to the Wyoming border. I say this, not because of the road itself, but because of the varied attractions that will tweak your inquisitiveness.

One summer in the seventies, with Montana as my destination, I stayed on I-70 and enjoyed a brief stay in St. Louis. Here I got the bright idea to emulate that historical duo, Lewis and Clarke, and trace their famous expedition west. Most early explorers generally followed rivers when available. These waterways offered easy access to water for the animals, and an easier route. In the Lewis and Clarke trek, the Missouri River was the answer. It didn't take long before I realized that I was already off track, so the historical duo became history and I concentrated on my present route. Connecting to Rte 29, Tinker carried me north to the Sioux Falls, South Dakota, area and I-90. Following this interstate west for about 70 miles, I came upon the town of Mitchell (population about 13,000 in 1973).

While enjoying a modest repast, the young waitress inquired if I was there to visit the Corn Palace. "The what?" I asked, and she proceeded to describe what sounded like an interesting tourist attraction. Now I'm not one to spend much time on such attractions, but my curiosity was piqued and since it was nearby, off I went. My first sight, I found hard to believe. Here was this large building with colored spires and domes, and the facade decorated with (what else?) corn. I decided to take a closer look and as I approached, there was a tour group inside, so I joined them. As usual the guide was overflowing with the history, yearly events, etc. From him we learned the palace was established in 1892. Corncobs, grain, and grasses cover its walls. We could see that some of the interior walls were covered with murals, also made of corn and grasses. The Corn Palace attracts about 500,000 visitors a year and in September the annual, weeklong Corn Palace Festival is celebrated. Many of the ears of corn disappear as souvenirs for guests.

Having seen enough to satisfy me, I left the group, and as I strolled off, the tour guide called to me, "Don't stray too far as the bus will be leaving shortly." I answered "okay," and headed for Tinker.

Back on I-90, I headed west. The Interstate Highway system is not exactly a scenic route, but the system did serve a great need. After approximately 175 miles, I reached the town of Cactus Flats and an entry route to the Badlands National Park. This short side trip through the Badlands was well worth the time and effort. I'm sure the good Lord provided this area of uneven terrain, eroded buttes, and fossil beds, to keep the painters, sketchers, and shutterbugs busy. I chatted with one future Rembrandt and admired her artistic interpretations of the surroundings as she applied the final touches to her masterpiece. The road through the park provides parking areas with markers that explain the geology and identify the various fossils from the long-ago Oligocene epoch.

Now to me, geology is not an exciting subject but as I viewed, and experienced, the deposits and such explained in the markers, I changed my mind. Incidentally, near the entrance to this park there is, or was, a helicopter pad offering scenic flights over the park. I wanted to try it but was denied, as they require a minimum of two passengers and I was the only one available.

A short distance from the exit of the park, you'll run into the city of Wall. This quaint little town is located at the north "wall" of the Badlands Park, thus its name. It has a unique history. Briefly, the Wall Drug Store actually put this burg on the map. The proprietor of the pharmacy attracted visitors by placing signs along local highways. It proved successful, so he spread the effort to every state in the union and, eventually, even to the Arctic and the South Poles. At its peak, his often comical signs offering free ice, attracted over one million visitors to Wall Drug each year. The Highway Beautification Act in 1965 brought a sudden end to his barrage of signs. Eventually, after some intense political efforts, South Dakota did permit some of the signs to be restored. As the Wall Drug Store grew, so did the town. When I-90 bypassed Wall, naturally, the number of visitors dropped somewhat. When I visited Wall, it was an endless array of shops: souvenirs, greeting cards, a cafeteria, etc. The pharmacy counter was relegated to a small corner of the drugstore.

About fifty miles on I-90 West led me to Rapid City for an overnight stop. Since I had spent so much time enjoying the Corn Palace, Badlands National Park, and Wall City, it was time to call it a day. After checking in at a local motel, I took a short ride to Mt. Rushmore, souvenir shop included. Nothing had changed since my last visit so it was a very brief stay, and back to the motel for the usual needed shower and sound night's sleep.

An early departure from Rapid City found me on Rte. 16 in a southerly direction for about fifteen miles, and at this point I followed secondary roads through the Black Hills National Forest. Eventually the no-number, winding, twisting, narrow trail will entertain you with turns so sharp you can almost see yourself coming back, and also a glimpse of Harney Peak, the highest point in So. Dakota. Finally I arrived at the town of Lead (pronounced *Leed*) with the help of Rte. 385, and then Deadwood. Now just to make things more confusing, *lead* means "lode" or "vein of ore." The town of Lead was named for the famous Homestake lode. This lode produces, or did produce, more gold than any other gold mine in the Western Hemisphere. Wild Bill Hickok, Calamity Jane, and Preacher Henry Weston Smith were buried in nearby Mount Moriah (Boot Hill) Cemetery. Now on to Sturgis and Spearfish, via I-90. All are interesting smalltowns that seem to overflow with friendly, smiling people.

But now, back to the interstate to make up some of my lost time en route. I shouldn't say "lost time," because the past few days provided many more sights and experiences that I will add to my book of warm memories for the cold nights of winter. A short ways beyond Spearfish, I connected to the very scenic Rte. 24, which circles the northern section of the Black Hills Forest. After about fifty miles of exotic biking, off in the distance, appeared an unusual sight. This apparition, in the northeast section of Wyoming, looked like a towering rock. Naturally I headed for this pile of stone, and after about five miles of dirt and mud road, I arrived at what turned out to be the "Devil's Tower." At the entry gate, a young lassie hesitatingly asked if I would happen to be a senior. At her behest, I went to the office and after being proofed, I was given a senior citizen card, which entitled me to enter any national park for the nominal sum of one dollar. I later learned that the Devil's Tower was the first national monument.

It was accorded this honor by President Theodore Roosevelt in the year 1906. Since this tower of fluted volcanic rock rises 1,280 feet above the Belle Fourche River, it was used as a landmark by our early explorers on their journeys to the West. It can be seen from one hundred miles from certain angles.

The Indian tribes of the area had many tales to explain the origin of the Devil's Tower's. The Kiowa tell of the seven sisters and their brother, who were playing, when the boy suddenly turned into a bear and started to chase the girls. The sisters climbed up on a rock to escape, and prayed for salvation. In answer to their prayers, the rock grew higher and higher, offering them safety while the bear clawed long scratches in the sides of the rock, trying to reach them. Eventually the sisters were pushed into the sky and became the seven stars of the Big Dipper. If we believe this, then we should conclude that the brother became Ursa Major.

Well, enough of the lore of the land and on to my original destination. Following I-90 into Montana, the Big Sky Country, I continued northward until, just a short distance from Hardin, I took a brief detour to visit the Little Bighorn Battlefield National Monument. Scattered tombstones mark the spot where the many soldiers of General Custer's army died at the hands of Chief Sitting Bull's warriors. A brief photo-shoot and back to the interstate. About 150 miles past Billings and just short of Bozeman, I headed north on the delightfully scenic Rte. 89. Another 200 miles and I finally arrived at Great Falls for a relaxing week of R&R.

For the return trip, Rte. 15 South led me to Helena, Montana's state capital, and a connection to Rte. 287. This highway, and I should add, a very scenic one, took me to Three Forks for some quick photos of the source of the Missouri River. If you are interested, Three Forks is where the Jefferson, Madison, and Gallatin Rivers meet to form the Missouri.

And now here I am, over 2,000 miles from home and running out of time. As always, when short of time, head for the interstates and maintain the speed limit till you safely reach home. This I did, and following my well learned lessons of "don't drive when tired," I did arrive home safely.

While many roads do not make the top-ten as seen through the eyes of a biker, they still leave an indelible mark on our gray matter. You might classify them as the most challenging roads. Trails such as the Alcan to Alaska, the Pan-Am to Panama, and the Sahara Desert roads (or lack thereof), were not exactly designed with the pleasure of biking in mind. You might even call them "the most unfavorable ones." But they do represent a challenge, or maybe even a dare, and once we accept the challenge, and come out on top, the exhilaration and satisfaction are overwhelming. Of course, they took the fun out of the Alcan when they blacktopped it. As for the Pan-Am Highway, it's still a challenge, due mainly to the absence of any safety features such as guardrails, center lines, and warning signs. (For a long time, local civil wars also made parts of the highway a dangerous route. Check the current status of things in places such as, most recently, the Zapotec areas of Mexico.) My Spanish language deficiency and the border hassles increased the challenge. As I write this, I hope and pray that improvements have been made. As for Tunisia, with the shifting sands and the salt flats of the Sahara, I don't know if there is a solution.

If I had to briefly classify these three roads I would judge the Alcan as a physical effort requiring concentration, dedication, and determination. The Pan-Am is more a mental effort, and, of course, a knowledge of Spanish will help. The Saharan trails are a combination of both.

And then there are roads that leave a remembrance of a different nature. One time while heading to Frisco on Rte. I-80, I took a break in Reno, Nevada, and then shortly after passing north of Lake Tahoe came upon Donner Pass. It was still summer but I noticed the snow poles were still in place. These poles aid the snow plows, telling the operators where the roadside sits. The height of the poles, about twelve feet, intrigued me, and later, at a rest area, I mentioned this to a fellow traveler. He was an area resident and he filled me in on the heavy snowfalls in this area, and also Donner Pass and the Donner Party tragedy. As usual when I returned home and checked the big book, his story was confirmed, exactly. Donner Pass is a highway and rail pass about 7,000 feet above sea level in the sierras of California, near the Nevada border and northwest of Lake Tahoe. The Donner Party, as described by my fellow traveler and the smart book, was a party of immigrants heading for California, led by George Donner. They were trapped in a blinding snowstorm in the Sierras (1846–1847). Stranded and soon out of food, the situation quickly became desperate. Three search parties were sent to their rescue, led by Captain Sutter's guides, and they did manage to rescue 45 of 87 members of the party. Later it was learned that the desperation had become so great that the survivors resorted to eating the flesh of their dead comrades: cannibalism, a tragic episode in American frontier history.

IX.
Clubs and Associations

As you glide over the concrete slabs and macadam pathways, somewhere, you are bound to meet up with fellow bikers, most of whom belong to a club or association. Don't ask me why humans who are loners by nature—else why would they own vehicles designed to carry one person, or two at most—join groups or clubs. Kind of like a sun worshipper who goes to the beach and then puts up an umbrella to block the sun. While I prefer to ride solo and alone (solo = empty buddy seat; alone = no other bikes), I do have a high regard for 99% of motorcycle clubs. Basically, they all strive to improve the image of cyclists, an image that has been somewhat tarnished by some movies and a few so-called outlaw groups.

The legitimate clubs contribute to innumerable charities, are ever ready to aid fellow travelers, two- or multiwheelers, while instilling a great spirit of camaraderie one rarely finds in other associations.

Except for Tunisia, all my longer excursions have been solo trips, so the only time I ever made a reservation was when my wife was to meet me at a destination. My dear patient wife was definitely not a biker—in fact, she would hesitate to enter our garage if my bike was there.

During my cycling days, I did participate in the activities of two clubs. One was a local group called the North Haledon Mountaineers and the other was the aforementioned Motorcycling Doctors Association. Why was the local group called the Mountaineers? Because North Haledon has a peak called High Mountain which is all of 800 plus feet above sea level. Our western state visitors might sometimes chuckle at that but, actually, High Mountain is the highest point of land within 20 miles of the Atlantic coast, and as ships approach New York Harbor, High Mountain offers the first sight of land. (The land along the mountain's top was once bought by a nostalgic, grateful immigrant for this reason.)

The other club I belonged to was the MDA (Motorcycling Doctors Association.) This was a national group, and our annual meeting was held anyplace in the USA. It consisted of physicians, dentists, veterinarians, and members of the allied health fields. The meetings usually consisted of group rides through surrounding scenic areas, with frequent stops to enjoy local highlights, and of course lunch, and seminars of interest to all. The annual session always included a donation to a local charity. Since the MDA was not a money-oriented organization, all surplus funds made up the donation. Our MDA Members were not financially hurting, and I was aware of occasions when a particular charity struck a chord with one of our members and he would augment the club's gift in a quiet unassuming manner. This not only helped the local charity but also helped change the attitude of some people regarding those who enjoy motorcycling.

Most areas around the country had their local clubs and the Garden State has its share. Thus we were able to participate in an ample supply of poker runs, charity runs, etc. For those not familiar with such activities, a poker run is a competition among a group of clubs, each of whom pays an entry fee. All clubs meet at the starting point and await their respective starting time. At the assigned time the club proceeds along a marked route to a succession of five stations. At each stop, the club selects a card from a deck and at the end of the ride, usually a picnic area, turns in their poker hand. The club that presents the best poker hand is declared the winner.

The prize is usually nominal since the real winner is the local or national charity for whom the whole affair was dedicated.

New Jersey bikers had a unique problem. It seems that when the Garden State Parkway, which runs from the New York state border to the southern tip of Jersey in Cape May, was completed, the great intellectual powers that be dictated that motorcycles were not welcome—in fact, they were banned. Thus New Jersey gained the dubious distinction of having one of the rare highways in the world that banned motorcycles. However, this situation was corrected in mid 1970. (A similar ban on heavy trucks remained.)

When the Parkway announced the lifting of the ban on motorcycles, naturally, every club in the state had visions of being the first group to ride the Parkway. To solve this dilemma the officials assigned each club an entry near their home base. The North Haledon Mountaineers was assigned the northernmost entry. In fairness to all (maybe that should be "unfairness to all"), the time was set at 12:00 a.m. on a cold November night and as our group assembled and waited for the go-ahead signal, we froze. A reporter from one of the local newspapers was in the process of interviewing me, as the oldest biker in this group, when up rode a gent who was in his seventies. I was dropped like a hot potato, make that a cold potato. The older gent was likewise dropped when a lady in her mid seventies rode up to join us. She was the more newsworthy story—seems she was on a solo charity run. Her goal was to visit the capital of each state in the US. A monetary donation to her particular charity was pledged for each capital she reached. I never heard about her or her goal again.

At the stroke of midnight we entered the Garden State Parkway and, lo and behold, the authorities waved us into the headquarters building. All our complaints against the Parkway Commission suddenly disappeared as we enjoyed some very welcome hot coffee and doughnuts. Their generous hospitality was truly appreciated by all. Since all clubs entered at the same time, none of us had the bragging rights but we all nurtured an improved image of the current Parkway Board. After traveling the parkway many times, I must admit I have never experienced anything but courteous treatment from parkway personnel.

During my biking days there were numerous national clubs and literally thousands of local clubs. Add the brand-name clubs to this list and, by now I have lost count. As a BMW owner and a subscriber to the BMW magazine, I was an automatic member of the BMWOA (BMW Owners Association). Also popular was the Honda Goldwing Association, and God forbid that I should leave out the Harley Hogs, or as one Georgia Club called itself, the Harley Hawgs. Not to be outdone, another Georgia club claimed "Road Dawgs" as their moniker. I guess if you belong to a Georgia club you can freely enjoy the byways in red clay country. One time while traveling through Georgia I stopped to feed my thirsty gas tank, and I noticed a well-uniformed highway patrolman, who had been tailing me for a few miles, sitting in his car just staring at me. When I left, he followed, but after a few miles of very cautious riding he must have become bored and gave up. I did get his message.

A fellow biker from New York had a Georgia patrol officer pull alongside while he was refueling and question him about where he was going. When the biker replied that he was on his way to New York, he was told to get on his bike and keep going till he was out of Georgia. Please spare me any more concerning Southern hospitality.

Remembering these incidents, I never stop in Georgia on my many trips from Florida to New Jersey and back. Since Georgia is only approximately 110 miles north to south on I-95, I feed my tank and tummy before the Georgia border. I truly hope they have changed their attitude since my biking days.

Motorcycle clubs are as varied as the bikes and the people who ride them. The clubs can be divided according to brand, goals, activities, interest, political focus, and occupation.

All cycle clubs have definite goals and the Abate Association (American Bikers Aimed Toward Education) does a great job on the political, charitable, educational, or fraternal level. Many states have their own Abate organization, dedicated to preserving individual freedom and promoting safety. They support rider training and safety and educational programs, and raise funds for the less fortunate through charity runs and benefits. All members are encouraged to become active in their respective communities while working to protect the rights of all bikers through direct involvement in the political process. Abate is nonpartisan and welcomes all riders.

The Retreads Motorcycle Club International is a nonprofit, socially oriented organization of about 20,000 members throughout the world. They share two characteristics: an age of forty-plus and a love of motorcycling. The Retreads originated in California in 1969. I believe one George Spidell was the founding father. As I recall from my brief attachment to this group, there were no dues but donations were accepted to help defray expenses.

There are numerous clubs using the title of Christian Riders, some are independent while others are internationally connected. These noteworthy groups strive to spread the word of Christ, and this they do very efficiently in a quiet manner. I had the pleasure of meeting a member in Missouri and we traveled eastward together till we reached Kentucky. Here we shared lunch and went our separate ways. He, like others, spread the word by his living example.

Another group with branches in many states is the Blue Knights. This is a law enforcement motorcycle club that consists of full- and part-time law enforcement officers. They actively participate in, and sponsor, numerous fund-raising programs for the March of Dimes, American Cancer Society, and many local charities. They also strive to promote motorcycling safety, family recreation, and the pleasure of riding. Incidentally, I was an associate member of a North Jersey Blue Knights group, maybe because I met so many Smokies along the interstates.

Very often we see police and firemen mentioned in the same breath, mainly in life-saving efforts, so it follows, naturally, that the firemen should have their own cycle club, and that they do. Not surprisingly, the group is called the Red Knights. The Red Knights is composed of members of the fire services and family members who (surprise) ride motorcycles. Their aim is to promote safety, project a positive image of motorcycling, and enjoy the fraternity of firefighters. Although independent of other groups or organizations, it is AMA (American Motorcycle Association) sanctioned. Membership is open to career, volunteer, industrial, disabled, and retired members of the fire service.

Now that we have the Blue Knights and Red Knights among occupational clubs, how about black? Sure enough, we have the Black Knights, composed of riders in the funeral service profession.

The aforementioned AMA is one of the oldest cycle organizations in the United States. It was formed in 1924 to further the interests of all American bikers, while serving the needs of its members. In later years its membership grew to more than 200,000. The Government Relations Department of the AMA seeks out bad laws and antimotorcycle discrimination, and expends much energy and funds to correct these conditions. It is the largest motorcycle sports sanctioning body and oversees more than eighty national-level racing events. These include supercross, high-bank track (Daytona), dirt-track racing, and hill climbs.

On one occasion, while enjoying a nice comfortable ride down in Texas, I had occasion to meet up with two bike clubs. A sudden downfall accompanied by thunder and lightning forced me to seek shelter under the next overpass. I dug out my rain gear (I don't know why, since I was already soaked). Visibility was about zero and cars began to share my shelter. The occupants of one car opened their door and invited me to sit in, out of the blowing rain, but I was already wet and not wishing to mess up their car, I politely turned down their thoughtful offer. This was not unusual since on at least two other occasions I had been invited to share lunch or dinner with folks traveling via car or camper. What was unusual in this case was the fact that this was in Texas, and Texans, generally speaking, have not been noted for kindness to blacks or Mexicans, and this car's occupants were an African American family who would have been totally justified in ignoring a soggy old white man, but they didn't.

When the rain lessened, I carried on to the next town in search of fuel, room, shower, and food in that order. I pulled into a gas station and refueled, and since there was a nice motel located behind the station, I took a shortcut through the back of the station. Not a bright idea, as the heavy rain had turned the ground into a quagmire and Tinker's front wheel sank to the hub. Before I could even search for help, a fellow biker and a couple from California in a pickup truck came to my aid. With a rope tied to Tinker's back rack, the pickup pulled my bike from the mire as the bikers and I, knee-deep in mud, steadied Tinker.

In appreciation for their generous help, I offered to sport them to dinner. The couple from California, anxious to get going, said thank you, and took off with their motorcycle safely tucked in the bed of the pickup. Incidentally, they were members of the Helping Hands M.C. Club. They surely lived up to their moniker. The other biker likewise turned down my offer as he was to meet family at the motel. Knowing their room number, I did return from dinner with a bottle of wine, which they accepted.

This particular biker happened to be a member of the Christian Riders.

Having had so many contacts with kind, helpful travelers has made me more aware of others in need of help. Even now as a four-wheeler I feel compelled to stop and offer aid to a stranded motorist or biker, whether it be for a jump start, gas, or whatever. One bright sunny day while cruising down one of Jersey's minor highways near my hometown, I came upon an elderly gent pushing his car as his young daughter, or maybe granddaughter, guided the vehicle down the emergency lane. I pulled up and, as I suspected, they had run out of gas. The nearest service station was about two miles away, so I offered to get the fuel and help restart the engine. Off I went, and since the station was on the opposite of the divided highway I made an illegal turn through a break in the cement divider. As I entered the station, so did Smokey Bear, who promptly informed me of my infraction. When he heard my explanation, he led me back to a legal turn and used his flashing lights while I emptied two gallons of fuel into the tank. Since gasoline at this time was relatively cheap and since the understanding officer had spared me a ticket, I refused payment for the fuel. The startled motorist, after repeated attempts to pay, and after a million thanks, drove off. I thanked the officer for his kindness and understanding and, likewise, rode off.

Most people look on motorcycling as a male milieu. Not true. The following is only a partial list of women's clubs and associations: The Motor Maids, Spokes-Women M.C., Women on the Road, Women on Wheels, Pony Express, Ebony Queens. Add to this list the numerous international women's clubs and you can see that it's not just a male sport. The Spokes-Women M.C. is worthy of a brief rundown. They believe in sharing the roads with all motorists in a neutral, non-judgmental, and safe manner. The club believes these goals can be realized through personal conduct, dressing wisely and safely while participating in the sport, riding in a safety-conscious and alert manner, and motorist education.

The club does not involve itself in any political issues. Members are free to participate in any personal or political issue, but not as representatives of Spokes-Women M.C. Inc. They maintain an active ride schedule throughout the year by participating in rallies, poker runs, swap meets, and cross-country touring. They have some members who also participate in the Polar Bear Club that rides each Sunday throughout the winter months.

The Spokes-Women M.C. was founded as the New Jersey Chapter of the American Women Road Riding Alliance, a national club. The N.J. chapter voted to separate from the national club and regroup locally under the new name and logo. The logo, which resembles spokes in the wheel of a bike, is actually a quilting pattern called the Mariner's Compass and represents the many points of the compass to which they ride.

Every year they organize charity fund-raising efforts and direct 100% of the proceeds to support agencies that are dedicated to the lives of women and children. Over the years they have donated thousands to the Juvenile Diabetes Foundation, Women's Crisis Services, Breast Cancer Foundation, Anderson House (N.J.), as well as Rider Education of New Jersey. They have full contact information at www.spokes-women.org/whoweare.html.

When you look over the names of the thousands of organizations around the world, it becomes apparent that names usually identify with their purpose. They are diverse and some have whimsical, humorous, or unusual names. A few examples: North American Nude Motorcycle Riders Association, Iron Butt Association, East Texas Wild Pigs (police and firemen), Booze Fighters Association, Choir Boys LEMC Texas (law enforcement), Grumpy Old Bikers, and finally, Rusty Nuts Motorcycle of New Zealand (a long-distance touring club). The Satyrs were the first gay motorcycle club, founded in Los Angeles in 1954, followed by the Sirens in New York City.

Many groups have a spiritual theme to their activities: Chariots for Christ, Christian Bikers Network, Cycle Disciples, Riders of the Cross, Rolling Hope, Christian Riders Ministry, and the aforementioned CMA (Christian Motorcycle Association).

When we refer to motorcycles as "two-wheelers," we are neglecting our comrades who travel via sidecars and trikes. These are three-wheelers. I had the pleasure of riding a few miles with a triker who had his three-wheeler powered by a Porsche engine. The sidecar advocates naturally have their own organizations, mostly in Europe. Among the U.S. clubs are the United Sidecar Association, Sidecar Racing Association, and Leading Links Motorcycle Club.

Not to be outdone, the Trikers include among their clubs the BTW (Brothers of the Third Wheel). The sole purpose of the BTW is to put trikers in touch with other trikers, to exchange ideas, help each other, and create friendships. They host an international "Trike-In" each August, in conjunction with Sturgis Bike Week, in South Dakota.

This brief summary is but a sampling of the ever-growing national and international motorcycle clubs and associations, many of which I have come in contact with along the byways. The members of all these clubs are dedicated bikers who, while enjoying the sport, devote innumerable hours to their favorite charities. They also do their best to promote the proper image of bikers and thus counteract the stereotype created by the movies and some goofy writers striving to create the sensational. Members of the biking fraternity do their job by good example.

What does the future hold for bikers? More cc's? More horsepower for what? Will the old-fashioned way of just cruising cross-country survive the faster option of flying? Chain drive, shaft drive, or maybe belt drive? (I believe belt drive was tried in 1980.) Improved torque, fancier accessories? Changes in weather gear?

I know this is only a brief summary of motorcycling clubs and I apologize for the multitude that this short description missed.

X.
Advice

For those teens who have dreams of biking just as soon as they are old enough to obtain a license, I say, slow down. To the parents, I say, keep your young ones off the street motorcycles until they have driven a car for at least one year. My own sons rode trail bikes long before they ever had an auto license. Riding the trails gave them great experience handling those bikes, but I still insisted, "no street bikes until you have driven a car for one year." Most accidents involving autos and cycles are explained by the motorist stating, "I didn't see him." And after driving an auto for a year you'll soon realize that motorcycles, while sometimes easy to hear, are difficult to see. That blind spot in the car's rearview mirror appears to grow larger as the trailing vehicle gets smaller. Be aware.

So now, assuming your energetic, maybe wild, teen, has discovered the problems of cars and bikes sharing the same road, what next? Numero Uno, take a good safety course. As for myself, I lucked through many miles aboard many bikes, and then while attending an annual meeting of the MDA (Motorcycling Doctors Association), in Missouri, we were offered the Motorcycling Safety Course. An interesting film and lecture session was followed by a hands-on training period. This included braking, steering, countersteering, cornering, and some seemingly minor points that suddenly become major in certain situations. Even though I was in my late fifties, I still learned new survival tricks. After a couple of miles up and down the highways you'll learn even more, definitely enough for you to realize that you'll never know it all. You will also learn that this beautiful, enjoyable toy can suddenly become a deadly weapon.

Items you may find helpful in certain conditions include a good rain suit, for sure as hell you are going to encounter rainy days when you must keep going. If you are heading west and the storm is going east, or vice-versa, seek an overpass and sit it out. If you are only a short distance from home, any old plastic will shed water. But if you are a serious biker, invest in a well-fitted Gore-Tex outfit. At one of our MDA meetings, I met a rep from a company that produced about the best and most expensive rain suit available. For a mere $275 he provided me with the most efficient get-up possible. The most expensive suit I have ever owned, including my fancy tux. This gentleman spent the best part of an hour measuring my body dimensions and a few weeks later delivered a custom-made classic. This Gore-Tex suit permitted sweat to escape from within while repelling the rain. (Since sweat occurs in single molecules, it can escape through the pores of Gore-Tex, and since rain falls in groups of molecules it cannot penetrate the small pores of Gore-Tex). It was designed to give me ample arm and leg movement. It also featured a very important item, a reflective stripe down each arm and leg, and also across the back. When I look back on the years of protection provided by this rain suit, I must admit it was an investment worth every dollar I spent. Speaking of reflective materials, you should always wear some sort of reflective vest or jacket to help motorists see you, especially at dusk.

An old cliché says, "Know the road, read the road, ride the road." Keep this in mind and you will increase the enjoyment of your biking days. That ugly black line down the center of each lane is the oil dripping from cars and trucks. When mixed with rainwater, it becomes very slippery. If you spot a large, circular, dark area in the road, it means there is a bump coming up—again, slippery when wet. In ten minutes of steady rain, the road, although wet, will be safe to ride. So, I repeat, sit and wait. Also be wary of those grated drawbridge crossings, rain grooves, and wide white-painted symbols indicating left turns, etc., that all seem to be designed to cause you to lose control of your bike. The answer—slow down.

I assume, by now, you have ridden trail bikes and thus have gained some sort of expertise in handling these cantankerous machines. Just don't go out and spend dad's (or your own) last buck on one of those high-priced, overloaded, overweight showpieces. Start out with a moderate-sized (and priced) machine, something below the 500cc level, and don't open it up when you hit the road, as they can literally fly. Of course a few visits from Smokey Bear will cure your urge to fly.

Trail bikes, by the way, are excellent alternatives for youngsters gravitating toward motorized two-wheel action. The two-wheelers offer great physical exercise, while honing skills such as hand-eye coordination, making quick judgments, and mechanical know-how. Time spent repairing broken pedals and other minor repairs, plus the hours doing odd jobs earning money to pay for replacement parts, all help to keep the young ones off the street, not on it. Naturally, a few bumps and bruises will speed up the learning process.

Too many people think bikers wear leathers and boots for the "macho" effect. Nothing could be further from the truth. Smart riders wear leather and boots for protection (don't animals wear leather for the same reason?), not only from the elements but also in case of that inevitable spill. Helmets, in my humble opinion, are a must. I get a chill when I see a biker cruising down or up the highway wearing a tee-shirt, shorts, no helmet, and many times, a passenger, in similar garb, perched upon the buddy seat. They're probably in a hurry to discover "road rash" first hand. Even through the heat of the Central American countries and the hot Saharan Desert I wore helmet and boots, and while I did shed the heavy leather jacket, I wore full-sleeve coverage and gloves. The driving gloves protected my tender hands from the burning sun. In the Sahara my European fellow bikers did likewise.

The bike—the only thing between you and oblivion. In order to increase the odds of survival in your favor, allow me to offer a few suggestions. Keep your bike well tuned, with good, properly inflated rubber. Good brakes, obviously, are very important, but more important is how you apply them. If you have front disc pads and rear band brakes, get the feel of proper pressure for each. Unlike your car, where you can slam down on the pedal and all four wheels react equally, your two wheeler, with front hand disc brake and rear foot band-brake pedal, will treat you differently. For starters, you might try 75% rear pressure and 25% front pressure, then adjust to you and your bike's liking. And make sure the directional signals are working.

A windshield is a great aid in all kinds of weather, but avoid those fork-mounted shields. At higher speeds they can become an oscillating headache, possibly leading to loss of control. Just maybe, you can learn from my own stupid experience. One day, after tuning up Tinker, I was anxious to test my handiwork. So I took Tinker out on one of our local highways. On a deserted stretch of the highway I opened it up. As I hit 100-plus mph the front wheel began to oscillate severely, due to the effect of the wind on my bar-mounted fairing. I eased back on the throttle in the hope the bike would calm down, but still the speed increased. At this point I was looking for a good place to lay it down, but the bike began to level off, and slow a little. At about 75 mph, it steadied. Spend the extra buck and go for a frame-mounted fairing, such as the Windjammer. Of course, a more intelligent solution is to avoid the high speeds that encourage such situations.

Crash bars are very helpful in protecting your valuable engine. Embarrassing as it may be, some time or other you are going to drop your bike. One time (make that a few times), I pulled up to my garage, lowered the sidestand, and sheepishly watched as Tinker fell over: I hadn't properly secured the sidestand. On another occasion, my buddy and I pulled up to a red light, he put his left foot down as usual as he came to a stop, but this time his foot slipped on the gravel on the road, and over he and his bike went. The solution is to be aware of what's around you.

Most people can't imagine a quiet motorcycle. Yes, there is such an animal—in fact there are many. I've had cars move into my path as I started to pass because the motorist couldn't see or hear me. Both my Honda and BMW were too quiet, so I attached an air horn and used it before passing any vehicle.

Be careful who you follow. Dump trucks, even with their garbage covered, still manage to eject debris that seems to be aimed at your face or body. Eighteen-wheelers are notorious for shedding large chunks of rubber from their recapped or retreaded tires. Always leave enough room for an escape route. When following trucks and pickups that are probably carelessly loaded with all kinds of baggage, leave plenty of room to duck falling cargo. Also, avoid tailgating, especially cars pulling small trailers with those tiny trailer wheels—they have a nasty habit of losing a wheel or suffering a flat. When the way is clear, pass them.

If and when you feel ready for an overnight jaunt, what next? First select your destination and how many days or weeks you will be on the road. Even if you intend to motel it, it's still a good idea to carry a sleeping bag, or at least a ground cover and a pup tent, just in case. If your route takes you south of the border or any tropical area, forget the tent and carry a light hammock, unless you enjoy the company of creepy, crawling creatures such as ticks, land crabs, ants, and worse. And make sure you keep the insect repellent handy.

A tank bag is useful for items such as sunglasses, camera, maps, and any other small articles you feel are necessary. Use your saddlebags for, maybe, four sets of underclothes and any dress wear you desire. It's a good idea to carry a small bottle of cold-water detergent for your laundry duties. I always carried a light jacket and dress shirt so I could feel dressed up in preparation for my martini and dinner, not necessarily in that order. One time after a grimy check-in at an upscale hotel, shower, and change of clothes, I checked with the desk regarding dinner. The lady politely asked if I was a guest at the hotel. After showing my room key she coyly remarked how different I looked.

All my bikes had tube tires, so I carried a spare tube for each wheel. My gear also included an air pump and an inflation canister to handle small tire leaks, spray lubricant for chain-driven bikes, spare clutch and brake cables, and extra bulbs for tail- and headlights. The clutch and brake cables can be attached to the active cables, leaving only the ends unattached. In case of a broken cable (and they do break), only the connection need be attached. A great time-saver. For added comfort, I added an inflatable seat cover. You just inflate by mouth to the desired comfort level and away you go. Your gluteus maximus will also appreciate it.

If your tour takes you into Mexico and points south, be prepared for a siege of turista, Toltec two-step, or Montezuma's revenge, commonly known as diarrhea. Part of my arsenal on the trip through Central America was that tiny white pill called Lomotil. Tiny but very effective, as I found out in Mexico and Tunisia.

While Mexico holds the dubious honor of "Turista Capital of the World" in the minds of many, I must inform you that, as of 1983, Tunisia was the more rightful holder of that title. My recollection is that Mexico was rated as a 30% experience for visitors, as opposed to a 50% Tunisian rate. I personally, sadly, experienced the condition in both countries, and also in Nicaragua. Most people will tell you to avoid the water, which may be good advice, but my personal feeling is that the true cause lies in general unsanitary conditions. In Mexico, I witnessed flies galore tasting the food, while customers waited to be served. In Tunisia the absence of sanitary efforts was quite apparent. Needless to say, when visiting any foreign soil, check the culture, customs, laws, restrictions, etc. And never get involved in religious or political discussions!

Please bear with me as I offer my last, and most important, bit of advice. I'm referring to drinking and driving, whether on two- or four-wheelers. Keep in mind that each alcoholic drink (and that includes beer) impairs your reaction time to some degree. Consider this: A stupid kid on a bicycle pulls out in front of you. Right or wrong, could you live with the horror of fatally injuring some youngster because you had just one more for the road?

And now that your bike, properly insured, is in perfect condition and you are properly attired, and you are aware of all road and weather conditions, what next? Well, rather than burden you with any more preaching, why not just read the following prayer:

"O God, I thank Thee for the marvel of a motorcycle, alive and powerful at the touch of my hands and feet, a thing of tremendous possibilities—wonderful, or terrible!

Help me to achieve the skill that will control it completely and wisely, like a tool shaping a better life for me and those around me.

I thank Thee for the promise of adventure that is mine each time I start: the thrill of the open road, far places, strange sights, new 'neighboring.'

Make me aware, as I drive the streets of my town—signaling, stopping, waiting, turning, and zooming ahead—that I do not have to do merely with trucks, taxis, cars, bicycles, pedestrians, but—with people!

People such as I know and touch as I walk the sidewalk and enter the homes of my neighborhood; people such as I am . . . making mistakes, perhaps, but not really wanting to.

Because I like people and know how important is their happiness, and how precious they are to Thee, . . . let me be alert, courteous, patient, considerate of the rights of others on the road, gracious enough to give up some of my own, and always careful, realizing that another's pain would destroy my pleasure, another's loss would rob my gain, and the life I save is just as precious as my own. Amen."

You know this world of ours consists of spectators and participants, so now, hop on your own version of "Tinker" and be a participant. Enjoy the wonderful world of motorcycling, and as you delight in the fall colors, especially in the northeast, remember, those pretty colors are short lived. All too soon they become fallen leaves—add a little soft rain and suddenly you have a slippery road. I'm sure you already know the answer: "Slow down." Finally, ride safe, and always stand ready to aid stranded fellow travelers, be they two-, three-, or four-wheelers.

Dedication

This literary effort would not have been possible without the support, help, and patience of numerous people. Foremost on the list was my wife of thirty-eight years, Elsie. She was blessed with the patience of the Biblical Job, and I'm sure she needed it to tolerate my meanderings. This dedication must also include my four sons, Joseph, Mark, David, and Robert. Their maturity, obedience, and respectfulness made fatherhood a pleasure. I thank them and their mother for making my life worthwhile. Six years after the demise of Elsie, I married another patient soul named Terri. She was not a motorcycle enthusiast, but I did manage to entice her aboard on a couple of occasions. Terri flew to most of our MDA meetings and enjoyed the company of the other members. Finally, when you have biked many miles, you are bound to meet more than a few fellow travelers, most of whom enter your life quickly, and disappear just as quickly. But some do leave an indelible impression on your life. [Note: The author passed away in the summer of 2007.]

Bibliography

California Missions, D. Krell
Central America, Doug Richmond
Compton's Encyclopedia, 1998 edition
The Desert: A Rendezvous with God, Rev. Mark Giordani
Fray Junípero Serra, Mark Brunnelle
Life and Times of Fray Serra, Msgr. Francis Weber
Tikal, William R. Coe
Tunisia, Michael Tomkinson
Victims, The, Gratton and Venice Puxon